LONGMAN
KEYSTONE

BUILDING BRIDGES

Kaye Wiley

PEARSON
Longman

Building Bridges

Copyright © by Pearson Education, Inc. This program was formerly published as *Shining Star*, Introductory level.

Pearson Education, 10 Bank Street, White Plains, NY 10606

Staff credits: The people who made up the Longman Keystone Building Bridges team, representing editorial, production, design, manufacturing, and marketing are John Ade, Rhea Banker, Liz Barker, Kenna Bourke, Diane Cipollone, Amanda Rappaport Dobbins, Johnnie Farmer, Warren Fischbach, Patrice Fraccio, Geraldine Geniusas, Charles Green, Aliza Greenblatt, Henry Hild, Ray Keating, Lucille M. Kennedy, Ed Lamprich, Linda Moser, Rebecca Ortman, Liza Pleva, Bill Preston, Edie Pullman, Tania Saiz-Sousa, Chris Siley, Jane Townsend, Lauren Weidenman, and Paula Williams.

Text design and composition: Kirchoff/Wohlberg, Inc.
Text font: 12.5/16 Minion

Acknowledgments: See page 287

Illustration and photo credits: See page 287.

Library of Congress Cataloging-in-Publication Data
Wiley, Kaye.
    Longman keystone: building bridges / Kaye Wiley.
    Formerly catalogued as Shining star: introductory level / Kaye Wiley
        p. cm.
    ISBN 0-13-207691-8 -- formerly catalogued as ISBN 0-13-111285-6
    1. English language -- Textbooks for foreign speakers --
    Juvenile literature. 2. Readers (Secondary)
    [1. English Language -- Textbooks for foreign speakers.
    2. Readers.]
    I. Title
    PE1128.M3326 2004
    428.6'4---dc22
                        2003023648

ISBN-13: 978-0-13-207691-3
ISBN-10: 0-13-207691-8

Printed in the United States of America
2 3 4 5 6 7 8 9 10—DWL—12 11 10 09

Consultants and Reviewers

Contents

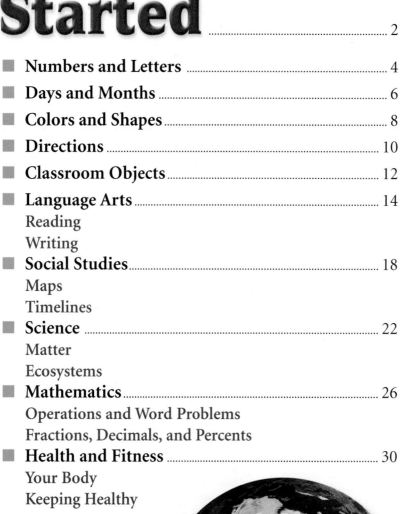

UNIT 1

Journeys

UNIT 2

Hidden Forces

UNIT 3

Play Ball!

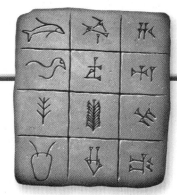

UNIT 5

The Power of Words

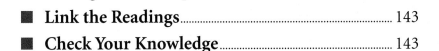

UNIT 6

Exploring the Senses 144

x

UNIT 7

The World of Plants

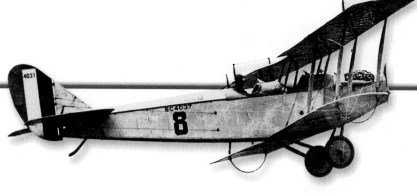

UNIT 8

Wings

PART 2

PUT IT ALL TOGETHER

HANDBOOKS AND RESOURCES

Dear Student,

Welcome to LONGMAN
KEYSTONE
BUILDING BRIDGES

This program will help you learn English for success in school. Some of the readings are about science and social studies. Other readings are about literature and culture. All of the readings have pictures to help you understand the text.

Before you begin each reading, look at the title and the pictures. Then read the list of Key Words. Ask yourself if you already know something about the topic. Then, as you read, stop and ask questions about what you are reading. Use the Reading Strategies. They will help you understand what you read. After you finish reading, discuss your ideas.

Each literature selection has a short play after it. The play retells the story that you read in the literature selection. You and your classmates can have fun speaking the different parts and rereading the story as a drama. You can also listen to recordings of all of the stories and plays.

The end of each unit has writing activities. Writing skills are a very important part of *Longman Keystone Building Bridges*. The writing activities will help you practice your grammar skills and learn to organize your ideas.

As you read and write more English, the world of school will open up for you. May you soon become a shining star in all your classes!

Kaye Wiley

◀ **Kaye Wiley is an ESL teacher and writer from New Haven, Connecticut.**

1

Getting Started

In this unit, you will learn and review numbers, letters of the alphabet, days of the week, and months of the year. You will talk about colors and shapes, and places and things in school.

Later, you will read and write a folktale. You will also learn how to read and use maps, timelines, diagrams, and a graph. Finally, you will use math skills to solve equations and word problems.

Are you ready? Let's get started.

OBJECTIVES
LANGUAGE DEVELOPMENT
Reading/Writing:
- Numbers and letters
- Days and months
- Colors and shapes
- Places in school
- Classroom objects

Listening/Speaking:
- Greet and introduce
- Talk about daily activities
- Give directions
- Describe locations

ACADEMIC CONTENT
- Language arts vocabulary
- Social studies vocabulary
- Science vocabulary
- Mathematics vocabulary
- Health and fitness vocabulary

Numbers and Letters

A. Listen and read.

Nina:	Good morning. What's your name?
Mrs. Schmidt:	My name is Mrs. Schmidt.
Nina:	How do you spell your last name?
Mrs. Schmidt:	It's S-c-h-m-i-d-t.
Nina:	How long have you been a teacher?
Mrs. Schmidt:	Fifteen years.
Nina:	Thank you.

B. Learn capital and lowercase letters.

Aa Bb Cc Dd Ee Ff Gg Hh Ii Jj Kk Ll Mm Nn Oo Pp Qq Rr Ss Tt Uu Vv Ww Xx Yy Zz

C. Learn these numbers and words.

Cardinal Numbers

1	one	**11**	eleven	21	twenty-one	**40**	forty
2	two	12	twelve	**22**	twenty-two	50	fifty
3	three	**13**	thirteen	23	twenty-three	60	sixty
4	four	14	fourteen	24	twenty-four	**70**	seventy
5	five	15	fifteen	**25**	twenty-five	80	eighty
6	six	**16**	sixteen	26	twenty-six	90	ninety
7	seven	17	seventeen	27	twenty-seven	**100**	one hundred
8	eight	18	eighteen	**28**	twenty-eight	1,000	one thousand
9	nine	**19**	nineteen	29	twenty-nine	500,000	five hundred thousand
10	ten	20	twenty	30	thirty	**1,000,000**	one million

D. Write the words for each of these numbers in your notebook.

13: _thirteen_

27: _____

71: _____

55: _____

42: _____

100: _____

38: _____

66: _____

60: _____

19: _____

1,000,000: _____

1,000: _____

86: _____

99: _____

11: _____

500,000: _____

E. Play this game with a partner. Look at the alphabet chart. Partner 1 reads five letters to Partner 2, for example: *K, A, V, G, L.* Partner 2 then writes the five letters in alphabetical order on a sheet of paper. Take turns. Check your answers.

Days and Months

A. Listen and read.

Luis: Hi, Sara. What day is it today?

Sara: It's Monday, July 7th. My basketball game is tonight. Do you want to come, Luis?

Luis: Sure. See you later!

B. Learn these numbers and words.

Ordinal Numbers

1st	first	**11th**	eleventh	**21st**	twenty-first	**40th**	fortieth
2nd	second	**12th**	twelfth	**22nd**	twenty-second	**50th**	fiftieth
3rd	third	**13th**	thirteenth	**23rd**	twenty-third	**60th**	sixtieth
4th	fourth	**14th**	fourteenth	**24th**	twenty-fourth	**70th**	seventieth
5th	fifth	**15th**	fifteenth	**25th**	twenty-fifth	**80th**	eightieth
6th	sixth	**16th**	sixteenth	**26th**	twenty-sixth	**90th**	ninetieth
7th	seventh	**17th**	seventeenth	**27th**	twenty-seventh	**100th**	one hundredth
8th	eighth	**18th**	eighteenth	**28th**	twenty-eighth	**1,000th**	one thousandth
9th	ninth	**19th**	nineteenth	**29th**	twenty-ninth	**500,000th**	five hundred thousandth
10th	tenth	**20th**	twentieth	**30th**	thirtieth	**1,000,000th**	one millionth

C. Look at the calendar. Answer the questions about Sara's activities in your notebook.

Monday	Tuesday	Wednesday	Thursday
plays basketball	*reads a book*	*watches TV*	*cooks dinner*

Friday	Saturday	Sunday
washes the dishes	*goes to the movies*	*plays the guitar*

1. When does Sara watch TV?
  She watches TV on Wednesday.
2. When does she wash the dishes?
3. When does she cook dinner?

4. When does she go to the movies?
5. When does she play the guitar?
6. When does she read a book?
7. When does she play basketball?

D. Learn these words.

Months of the Year

January	February	March	April	May	June
July	August	September	October	November	December

 Complete the sentences about months in your notebook.

1. August is the ___eighth___ month of the year.
2. The new year begins in _____.
3. _____ usually has twenty-eight days.
4. November is the _____ month of the year.
5. I like the month of _____ best.
6. May is the _____ month of the year.

Colors and Shapes

A. Listen and read.

Martin: What color is Japan's flag?

Laura: Japan's flag is red and white.

Martin: What shapes are in it?

Nadia: It has a red circle inside a white rectangle.

B. Learn the colors.

red	pink	blue	purple	green	yellow
orange	brown	black	gray	white	tan

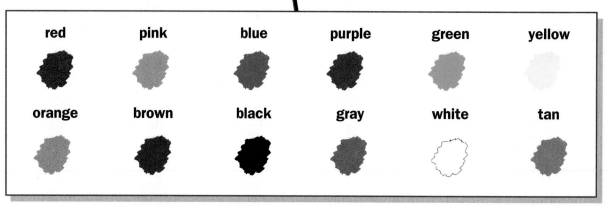

C. Learn the shapes.

circle	square	rectangle	triangle	star

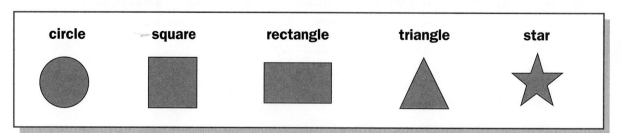

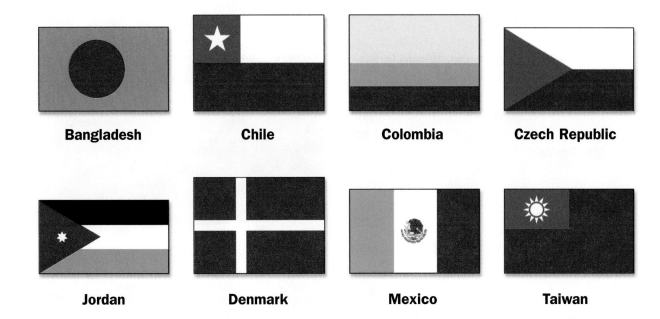

Bangladesh   **Chile**   **Colombia**   **Czech Republic**

Jordan   **Denmark**   **Mexico**   **Taiwan**

D. Look at the flags. Answer these questions in your notebook.

1. What color is Colombia's flag?
   Colombia's flag is yellow, blue, and red.
2. What color is Jordan's flag?
3. What shapes are in Denmark's flag?
4. Which flags have circles?
5. Which flags have squares?
6. Which flags have triangles?
7. Which flags have stars?
8. Which flags have rectangles?

E. Draw with a partner. Make a new flag. Use many shapes and colors.

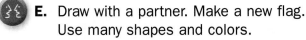

9

Directions

A. Listen and read.

Ms. Parker: Excuse me. Where is the main office?

Tara: Go in the main entrance. Turn left. Then go straight. It's across from the library.

Ms. Parker: Thank you.

B. Learn these words to give directions.

←	↑	→
Turn left.	**Go straight.**	**Turn right.**

next to   **between**   **across from**

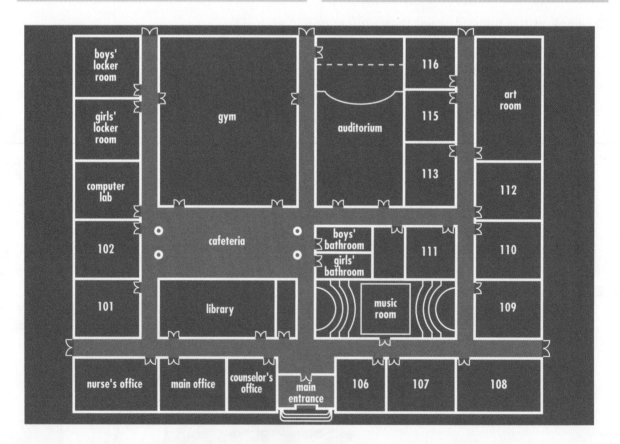

C. Write in your notebook. Give directions. Use the school map. Begin from the main entrance.

1. Where is the library?
   Turn left. Then go straight. It's across from the main office and the counselor's office.
2. Where is the cafeteria?
3. Where is the music room?
4. Where is the gym?
5. Where is the auditorium?

 D. Play this game with a partner. Ask each other questions.

1. What is across from the gym? *The cafeteria*
2. What is between the art room and the auditorium?
3. What is next to the library?
4. What is across from the counselor's office?
5. What is between the nurse's office and the counselor's office?

Classroom Objects

A. Listen and read.

Steve: What is that?
Carla: It's a globe.
Steve: What are those?
Carla: They're books.

B. Learn classroom words.

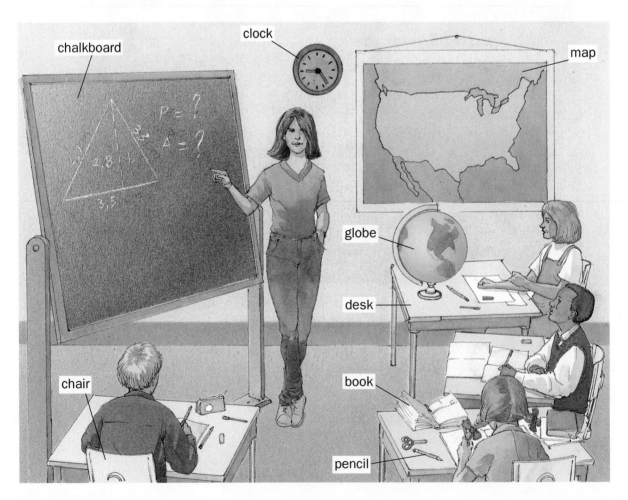

chalkboard

clock

map

globe

desk

chair

book

pencil

12

C. Write five sentences about objects in your classroom. Use numbers in your sentences.

> *There is one clock in my classroom.*
>
> *There are 32 chairs in my classroom.*

 D. Work with a partner. Look at the drawing on page 12. Ask and answer the questions.

1. What is across from the chalkboard?
2. What is between the chalkboard and map?
3. What color is the clock?
4. What color is the chalkboard?
5. What shape is the clock?
6. What shape is the map?
7. What shape is the globe?

Language Arts

Nonfiction is about real people, places, and events. Science and social studies texts are types of nonfiction.

READING STRATEGY

Find Main Idea and Details

When you read nonfiction, find the **main idea** and **details**.
- The main idea is the biggest or most important idea.
- Details are ideas or facts about the main idea.

 A. Read this social studies text.

Antarctica

The continent of Antarctica is very cold. An ice sheet covers most of the land. The average winter temperature is -60°C (-76°F). Few animals can live there all year. In the summer, animals such as penguins, whales, and seals come to Antarctica to eat food and to breed, or have babies.

 B. Copy this chart. Write the details about the main idea.

main idea

> Antarctica is very cold.

14

Fiction is about characters and events that writers make up. Myths, folktales, and short stories are types of fiction.

READING STRATEGY

Identify Characters, Plot, and Setting

As you read fiction, think about the **characters**, **plot**, and **setting**.

- The characters are the people or animals in the story.
- The plot is what happens in the story.
- The setting is the time and place of the story.

 C. Read this Native American folktale.

How Bear Lost His Tail

Many years ago in North America, Bear had a long tail.

One cold winter day, Bear saw Fox at the lake. Fox was sitting on the ice next to many fish. "How did you catch those fish?" Bear asked.

"With my tail," Fox lied. He wanted to fool Bear. Bear put his tail into the icy water. Soon Bear was asleep. Fox went home to eat his fish.

When Fox returned, Bear was still sleeping. "Bear!" Fox shouted. "Can you feel a fish on your tail?"

Bear jumped up, and his frozen tail broke off.

And that's why bears have short tails today.

 D. Read the folktale again. Answer these questions.

1. Who are the characters?
2. What is the plot?
3. What is the setting of the story?

A process is a way of doing something. Usually a process has a number of steps, or actions, that help you learn to do it.

 A. Read about the writing process.

The Writing Process

The writing process is a series of steps that help you write. Many writers use the writing process to think of ideas and then to organize, write, and revise their writing. Here are the steps.

Prewrite Before you can write, you need ideas. Brainstorming is a way of getting ideas. When you brainstorm, write down *all* the ideas you can think of about a topic. Make a list.

Look at your list. Choose the best ideas. Then make notes to organize your ideas.

Draft Use your notes to write your report or story. Write your ideas about your topic in sentences.

Edit Read your draft. Make sure your sentences are clear and easy to understand. Check your spelling and punctuation.

Ask another student to read your writing to check for mistakes.

Revise Rewrite your report or story. Add details to make the writing more interesting. Correct any mistakes.

Publish Share your writing with the class.

B. Read the notes the writer made before writing
"How Bear Lost His Tail."

	Notes for "How Bear Lost His Tail"
Beginning:	Bear had a long tail.
Middle:	Fox wanted to fool Bear. Fox said he had caught fish with his tail. Bear put his tail into the icy water. Bear fell asleep.
End:	Bear's frozen tail broke off.

 C. Compare the writer's notes with the folktale on page 15. Answer the questions in your notebook.

    1. How are the notes different from the folktale?

    2. How did the writer use the notes to write the folktale?

    3. Are the writer's notes mostly about character, plot, or setting? Explain.

 D. Write a folktale about something in nature, for example, "Why the Moon Is White." First, make a list of ideas in your notebook. Next, make notes to organize your ideas. Then write the folktale.

E. Trade folktales with a partner. Read your partner's story. Give your partner ideas for how to make his or her story better. Listen to your partner's ideas about your story. Then revise your story.

17

Social Studies

Social studies textbooks often have maps. Maps help you understand where people live and where events take place.

 A. Work in groups. Study the map below. Then answer the questions.

1. What countries are on the map?
2. What oceans are on the map?
3. Name three cities on the map.
4. Name two bays on the map.

B. Read about a compass rose.

   Many maps use a compass rose to show direction. This compass rose shows the directions north (N), south (S), east (E), and west (W).

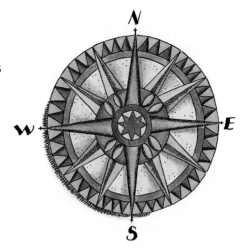

 C. Work with a partner. Study the map. Answer the questions.

1. What state is north of New Mexico?
2. What state is west of North Dakota?
3. What state is east of Georgia?
4. What state is south of Utah?

Timelines help you remember important dates and the order of events in history.

 A. Read this text. It tells about part of the history of California.

California, the Golden State

Native Americans were the first people to live in what is now California. Then, in the 1500s, Spanish explorers came to the land. At that time, Spain also controlled the territory where the country of Mexico is today.

In 1821, Mexico won its independence from Spain. As a result, California became a part of Mexico. Soon more people came to California. Some people sailed in ships around the tip of South America. Others traveled in wagons across the United States.

In 1846, Mexico and the United States fought a war. When the peace treaty was signed on February 2, 1848, California became a territory of the United States. Two weeks before, a man named James Marshall discovered something amazing near Sacramento, California. John Sutter, a Swiss settler, hired Marshall to help him build a sawmill. On January 24, 1848, Marshall saw shiny pieces of yellow metal in a stream by Sutter's Mill. They were pieces of gold!

Many people came to California to find gold. They were called "forty-niners" because they came in 1849. Soon people came from all over the world, including China and Australia. On September 9, 1850, California became the thirty-first state in the United States.

B. Look at the timeline. Answer the questions with a partner.

1500s	1821	1848	1850
Spanish explorers come.	Mexico wins independence from Spain.	Marshall discovers gold.	California becomes a state.

1. When did Spanish explorers come to California?
2. When did Mexico win its independence from Spain?
3. When did James Marshall discover gold?
4. When did California become a state?

 C. Make a timeline of other important dates in California's history or in the history of another state. Use the library or the Internet to find information.

James Marshall discovered gold at Sutter's Mill, near Sacramento, in 1948. ▶

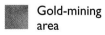 Gold-mining area

Science

MATTER

Everything you can touch or see is matter. Matter has three states, or forms: solid, liquid, and gas.

A. Read about the three states of water.

solid   **liquid**   **gas**

Three States of Water

Water is an important liquid. Water covers about 70 percent of the earth's surface. Your body is about two-thirds water. When water is in its liquid state, you can pour it. As a liquid, water takes the shape of its container. The water in the picture above takes the shape of the glass.

When water gets very cold, it freezes. It changes from a liquid to a solid. The freezing point of water is 0°C (32°F). Ice and snow are solid forms of water.

When water gets very hot, it boils. Then it changes from a liquid to a gas. This gas is called water vapor or steam. The boiling point of water is 100°C (212°F).

B. Work with a partner. Complete the sentences.

1. _____ and _____ are solid forms of water.
2. When water gets very hot, it _____.
3. The _____ point of water is 0°C.
4. Very hot water changes from a liquid to a _____.

C. Read about the water cycle.

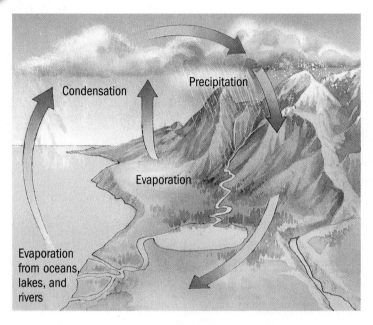

Condensation

Precipitation

Evaporation

Evaporation
from oceans,
lakes, and
rivers

The Water Cycle

The movement of water from the ground to the air and back is called the water cycle. In the water cycle, water changes its state as it moves. The sun heats water on the ground and changes it to water vapor. This change is called evaporation. Then water vapor moves up in the air and forms clouds. Water vapor cools in the clouds and changes into water drops. This change is called condensation. When the water drops become large enough, they fall from the clouds down to the ground as precipitation, such as rain or snow.

 D. Work in groups. Study the diagram again. Then answer the questions.

1. What is water called after it evaporates?
2. What happens to water vapor in clouds?
3. Name two kinds of precipitation.
4. Explain how water changes its state in the water cycle.

An ecosystem is all the living and nonliving things in an area. Living things include plants and animals.

 A. Read about the living things in an ecosystem.

Producers, Consumers, and Decomposers

There are three kinds of living things in an ecosystem: producers, consumers, and decomposers.

Most plants are producers. They produce, or make, their own food. Animals are consumers. Animals cannot make their own food. They consume, or eat, plants or other animals.

Fungi and bacteria are decomposers. Fungi are like plants, but they live in dark places. Mushrooms are examples of fungi. Bacteria are very tiny things that live in soil, air, and water. Fungi and bacteria decompose, or break down, dead plants and animals. They help the dead plants and animals become part of the soil.

Plants are producers.   Animals are consumers.   Fungi are decomposers.

B. Work with a partner. Match the words and their meanings.

_____ **1.** A consumer   **a.** makes its own food.

_____ **2.** A decomposer   **b.** eats plants and animals for food.

_____ **3.** An ecosystem   **c.** breaks down dead plants and animals.

_____ **4.** A producer   **d.** is all the living and nonliving things in an area.

C. Read about a food chain. Look at the drawing.

A Food Chain

The way food moves through an ecosystem is called a food chain. A food chain begins with a producer—a plant, such as grass. A small consumer, such as a mouse, eats the grass. Then a larger consumer, such as a hawk, eats the mouse. Decomposers, such as bacteria, break down the hawk when it dies. Its body becomes part of the soil.

 D. Work with a partner. Look at the pictures. In your notebook, number the pictures to make a food chain.

snake	grass	owl	grasshopper	toad
—	—	—	—	—

Mathematics

Use symbols and words to show addition, subtraction, multiplication, and division.

Operations:	addition	subtraction	multiplication	division
Symbols:	+	−	×	÷
Words:	plus	minus	times	divided by

 A. Read the examples of these four operations.

Addition

$$4 \qquad \text{or} \qquad 4 + 2 = 6 \qquad \text{or} \qquad \text{Four plus two equals six.}$$
$$+\,2$$
$$\overline{6}$$

Subtraction

$$8 \qquad \text{or} \qquad 8 - 3 = 5 \qquad \text{or} \qquad \text{Eight minus three equals five.}$$
$$-\,3$$
$$\overline{5}$$

Multiplication

$$6 \qquad \text{or} \qquad 6 \times 3 = 18 \qquad \text{or} \qquad \text{Six times three equals eighteen.}$$
$$\times\,3$$
$$\overline{18}$$

Division

$$\overset{2}{6\overline{)12}} \qquad \text{or} \qquad 12 \div 6 = 2 \qquad \text{or} \qquad \text{Twelve divided by six equals two.}$$

 B. Write the problems in your notebook. First write them in words. Then use numbers. Solve the problems.

1. Twenty-five plus eleven equals _____.
2. Thirty-seven minus twenty-two equals _____.
3. Twelve times ten equals _____.
4. Sixty divided by fifteen equals _____.

C. Read about word problems.

A word problem is a math problem with words and numbers. You can use addition, subtraction, multiplication, and division to solve word problems. Follow these steps:

1. Read the word problem carefully.

2. Ask yourself, "What operation do I use to solve the problem?"

3. Look for words in the problem that help you decide which operation to use.

4. Sometimes a picture can help you solve a word problem.

 D. Work with a partner. Read the word problems. Follow the steps above and solve each problem.

1. José is fourteen years old. José's sister is five years older than José. José's brother is three years younger than José. How old are José's sister and brother?

2. A redwood tree in California is about 111 meters tall. It is 18 meters taller than the Statue of Liberty in New York. How tall is the Statue of Liberty? (*Hint:* Look at the picture. Do you need to add or subtract to solve the problem?)

3. Kim has a box of oranges. The box has twenty-one oranges. Kim eats one orange each day. In how many weeks will Kim eat all the oranges? (*Hint:* How many days are in one week?)

4. Tom reads three books every week. How many books does he read in one year? (*Hint:* How many weeks are in one year?)

FRACTIONS, DECIMALS, AND PERCENTS

 A. A fraction is a number smaller than one. Read the examples.

 This is 1/2 (one-half).

 This is 3/4 (three-fourths or three-quarters).

 This is 4/5 (four-fifths).

A fraction has two numbers divided by a line. Look at the examples.

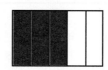

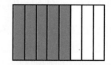

2/3 (two-thirds)   3/5 (three-fifths)   5/8 (five-eighths)

 B. In your notebook, write the fraction—numbers and words—for each picture.

1. _____ or _____

2. _____ or _____

3. _____ or _____

4. _____ or _____

C. A decimal is a number smaller than one. A decimal has a decimal point (.) and a number. For example, .3 and .25 are decimals. Read about the U.S. dollar.

The U.S. dollar is based on decimals. Ten pennies equals one dime. One penny is 1/10 of a dime. You can write the fraction 1/10 as the decimal .1. You say the fraction and the decimal the same way: *one-tenth.*

          =

Ten dimes equals one U.S. dollar. One dime is 10/100 of a dollar, or .10 as a decimal.

           =

D. A percent is a part of 100. A percent has a number and a percent symbol (%). For example, 10% means ten percent (of 100).

Fractions, decimals, and percents can show the same amount or part of something.

Fraction: 1/5 of the circle is blue. [1/5 = 1 divided by 5]

Decimal: .20 of the circle is blue. [1/5 = 20/100 = .20]

Percent: 20% of the circle is blue. [.20 × 100 = 20%]

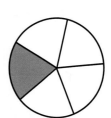

E. In your notebook, write the answer as a fraction, a decimal, and a percent.

Fraction: _____ of the circle is blue.

Decimal: _____ of the circle is blue.

Percent: _____ of the circle is blue.

Health and Fitness

Diagrams help you understand and remember important information. Many diagrams use pictures with labels, or words.

 A. Work in groups. Study the diagram. Then answer the questions.

1. What parts of the body help you see?
2. What parts help you write?
3. What part helps you smile?
4. What parts help you hear?
5. What parts help you run?
6. What part connects your foot to your leg?
7. What part helps you bend your arm?
8. What part helps you smell?

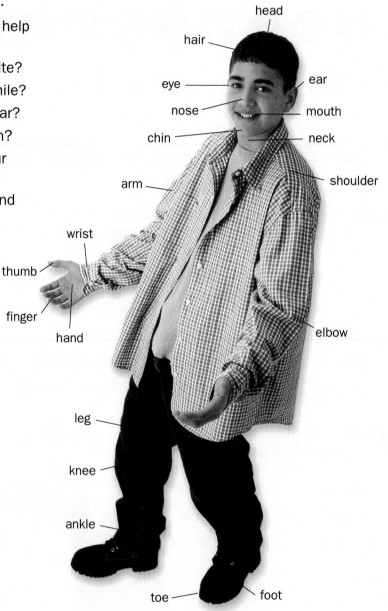

head
hair
eye
nose
chin
ear
mouth
neck
arm
shoulder
wrist
thumb
finger
hand
elbow
leg
knee
ankle
toe
foot

B. Read about physical exercise.

Physical exercise is good for your body. It helps your bones and muscles stay strong. Some people like aerobic exercise. Others enjoy sports such as golf or tennis.

A calorie is a unit for measuring how much energy your body gets from food. Exercise burns, or uses, calories to keep your body healthy and strong.

▲ Exercise helps keep you healthy.

C. Bar graphs compare information. Read the bar graph. It compares different activities. It shows how many calories each activity burns in one hour. Then answer the questions with a partner.

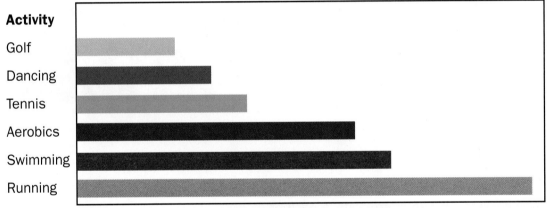

Exercise and Calories

1. Which activity uses the most calories?
2. Which activity uses the least calories?
3. Which uses more calories, swimming or dancing?
4. Which is your favorite activity? Explain.

KEEPING HEALTHY

You are what you eat. It is important to eat a variety of healthy foods every day. Do you have good eating habits?

A. Read the Food Pyramid diagram.

To keep healthy, eat more foods from the bottom of the pyramid. Foods from the top, such as candy and cake, have a lot of fat and sugar. Eat less of these foods.

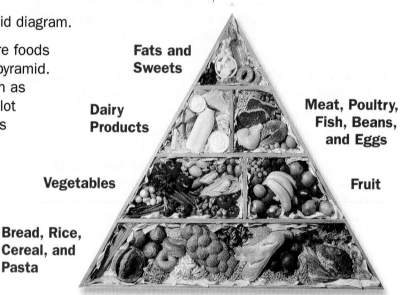

Fats and Sweets

Dairy Products

Meat, Poultry, Fish, Beans, and Eggs

Vegetables

Fruit

Bread, Rice, Cereal, and Pasta

B. Copy the chart in your notebook. Write what you eat in the chart. Compare charts with a partner.

My Food Diary	
Food Group	**Example**
Fats and sweets	cookies
Meat, poultry, fish, beans, eggs	
Dairy products	
Fruit and vegetables	
Bread, rice, cereal, pasta	

 C. Read about healthy habits.

A habit is something you do often or every day. Exercise and eating healthy food are two examples of good, or healthy, habits. Smoking and eating a lot of sweet and fatty foods are examples of bad, or unhealthy, habits.

 D. Copy the chart in your notebook. Work with a partner. Take turns asking questions about healthy habits.

Healthy Habits	Your Partner	You
Exercise every day		
Eat a healthy diet		
Wear a helmet when biking or skating		
Go to your doctor for check-ups		
Brush your teeth and visit your dentist		
Get plenty of sleep		
Keep yourself clean and neat		
Drink plenty of water		
Wear a seatbelt in the car		

E. Play this game in small groups. One person acts out a healthy habit. The first player to guess the habit gets to act out another habit. Play until everyone has a turn.

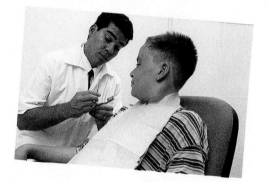

JOURNEYS

Some people do not live in one place. Instead, they move from place to place. These people are called nomads. The selection "Nomads" tells about how these people live. Some nomads live in the desert. The folktale "Jewel in the Sand" is about desert nomads.

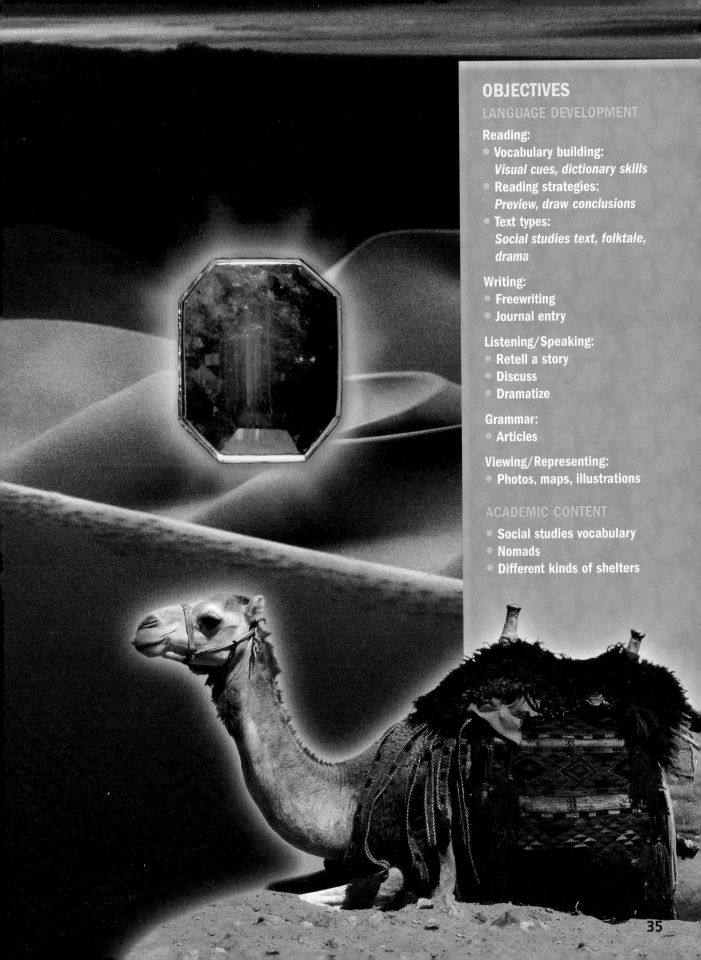

OBJECTIVES

LANGUAGE DEVELOPMENT

Reading:
- **Vocabulary building:**
  Visual cues, dictionary skills
- **Reading strategies:**
  Preview, draw conclusions
- **Text types:**
  Social studies text, folktale, drama

Writing:
- **Freewriting**
- **Journal entry**

Listening/Speaking:
- **Retell a story**
- **Discuss**
- **Dramatize**

Grammar:
- **Articles**

Viewing/Representing:
- **Photos, maps, illustrations**

ACADEMIC CONTENT

- **Social studies vocabulary**
- **Nomads**
- **Different kinds of shelters**

Prepare to Read

"Nomads" tells about real people. It is nonfiction. Nonfiction is factual information. You read it in textbooks. This nonfiction is social studies.

USE WHAT YOU KNOW

1. Why do some people live in tents?
2. What do you think the woman in the picture is doing?

LEARN KEY WORDS

buffalo
camels
desert
herds
nomads
tents

VOCABULARY

Look at the pictures and the captions, or words underneath the pictures. They will help you learn the words in the box. Write the meaning of each word. Then check your work in a dictionary.

▲ Some nomads live in the **desert**. They often travel with **camels**.

▲ **Nomads** move from place to place. These nomads from Mongolia (mon-GO-lee-uh) live in round **tents**. Mongolia is in Asia.

◀ The Sioux (SOO) people were nomads of North America. They hunted **buffalo**. The buffalo moved in groups called **herds**.

READING STRATEGY

Preview

To **preview** means to look at the pages before you read.

- Look at the headings in dark type.
- Look at all the pictures and maps.
- Try to guess what the text is about.

Nonfiction gives true information. "Nomads" tells about people who travel from place to place. Preview the pages. What do the pictures and headings tell you about nomads?

NOMADS

What Are Nomads?

Nomads are people who do not live in one place. They move from place to place to find food and water. They carry their homes with them on their **journeys**. In **prehistoric** times most people were nomads. They hunted animals and looked for seeds and plants to eat.

Are All Nomads Hunters?

Some nomads today are hunters, but most are herders. They travel with herds of sheep, goats, or camels. They look for places that have grass and water for their animals. These nomads often live in tents. They travel in large family groups called tribes.

---

journeys, long trips
prehistoric, before people
    started writing
    down history

**Woman herder with
long-haired lamb ▶**

▲ This cave painting shows prehistoric nomads hunting elk.

MAKE CONNECTIONS

1 How large is your family group? Count your family members.

2 Are there nomads in your home country? Explain.

Where Do Nomads Live?

Most nomads live on open land. Some live in the desert. Others live on **grassy plains**. In the past, nomads also lived in the ice and snow of the Arctic.

Who Are the Bedouins?

The Bedouins (BED-oo-inz) are desert nomads. They travel across the deserts of the Middle East and northern Africa. They have herds of camels. Camels are good desert animals because they can go many days without food or water.

Some Bedouins camp near water. Then they can keep horses, sheep, and goats. The women make tents and rugs from camel hair and goat hair. Bedouin families camp in groups called clans. The clan leader is called a sheik. Many clans together make a tribe.

---

grassy plains, large areas of land where grass grows

CHECK YOUR UNDERSTANDING

1. Why are camels good desert animals?

2. What do Bedouin women make from camel and goat hair?

3. What is a clan?

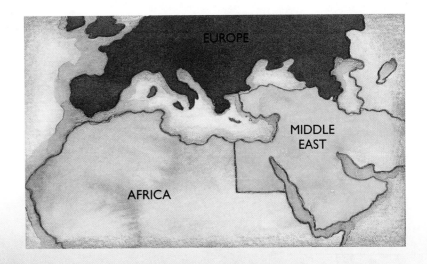

Bedouins traveling across the desert with camels and other animals ▼

39

Who Are Mongolian Nomads?

Mongolian nomads live in Asia. They travel with herds of horses, sheep, cows, and goats. They live in round tents called yurts. Yurts are made of wool from sheep. Yurts protect the nomads from bad weather.

Mongolian nomads are famous horseback riders. Men and women ride horses and shoot arrows for fun. Young children even learn to race horses.

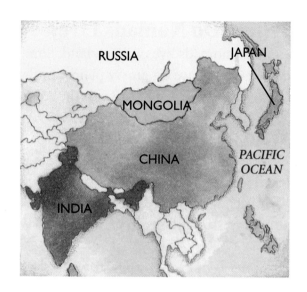

◀ Mongolian family in front of their yurts

◀ Mongolian children get ready for a horse race.

MAKE CONNECTIONS

1 What do you think it's like to live in a yurt?

2 What kinds of sports and races are there in your home country?

▲ Sioux hunters chasing buffalo

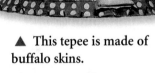
Sioux

Are There Nomads in North America?

There are very few nomads left in North America. Before 1850, there were many nomads. The Sioux, for example, hunted buffalo on the plains. They used buffalo meat for food. They made tents and blankets from buffalo skins. The tents were called tepees.

The Inuit, who live in the most northern part of North America, were also nomads. In summer they lived in tents by the sea and fished. In winter they hunted seals and polar bears. They used small boats called kayaks. Today most Inuit live in towns or villages. They are no longer nomads.

▲ This tepee is made of buffalo skins.

CHECK YOUR UNDERSTANDING

1 What animals did the Sioux hunt?

2 What animals did the Inuit hunt in the winter?

◀ Inuit hunting in a kayak

Inuit

Review and Practice

RETELL AND REVIEW

1. Tell a partner what you learned about nomads. Use the headings and the pictures on pages 38–41 to help you.

2. How did previewing the headings and pictures in "Nomads" help you get ready to read? Did you guess what the text was about? Explain.

COMPREHENSION

Write the sentences below in your notebook. Use the words in the box to complete the sentences.

buffalo	herds	~~nomads~~	tribes
camels	kayak	desert	yurt

1. People who travel from place to place are called _nomads_ .

2. Nomads often keep _____ of animals.

3. Some nomads live in the _____ .

4. A _____ is a round Mongolian tent.

5. Nomads travel in large family groups called _____ .

6. A _____ is a large animal that the Sioux hunted.

7. The Inuit fish in a boat called a _____ .

8. Many Bedouins travel with herds of _____ .

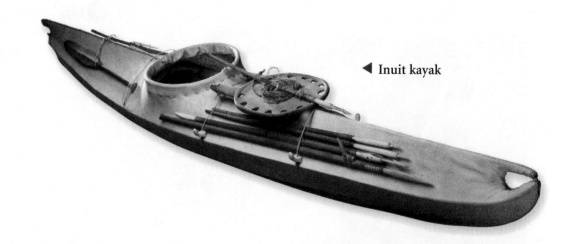

◀ Inuit kayak

42

Extension

DIFFERENT KINDS OF SHELTERS

A shelter is a place where people live. It is a home. It protects the people inside from bad weather. Look at the shelters below. How are they alike? How are they different?

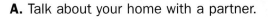

A. Talk about your home with a partner.

1. What kind of shelter is it?
2. How does it protect you from bad weather?
3. Draw a picture of your home.
4. Compare your home with the shelters shown on this page.

B. Find out more about shelters. Follow these steps:

1. Look at a map or globe.
2. Choose a country.
3. Find information about that country. Use the Internet or library books.
4. Read about the shelters or homes in that country.
5. Draw a picture of a home from that country.
6. Share your picture and the information you learned with the class.

Prepare to Read

"Jewel in the Sand" is a folktale. Folktales are stories that people, or folk, tell one another. Folktales began as oral stories, told by word of mouth. In time people wrote down the stories. Sometimes folktales teach a lesson. Sometimes people tell them just for fun.

TRY TO PREDICT

1. Where do you think the story takes place?
2. What do you think the story is about?

44

LEARN KEY WORDS

daughter
earrings
jewels
nephew
princess
uncle
welcomed

VOCABULARY

Look at the pictures and the captions. They will help you learn the words in the box. Write the meaning of each word. Check your work in a dictionary.

▲ This **princess** is wearing **earrings**. The earrings have **jewels** in them. A princess is the **daughter** of a prince or a king.

▲ The young woman **welcomed** the old woman into her tent.

◄ The man is the boy's **uncle**. The boy is the man's **nephew**. The man is the brother of the boy's mother or father.

READING STRATEGY

Draw Conclusions

To **draw** a **conclusion** means to decide something is true based on information. For example, you see someone wearing expensive clothes. You might draw the conclusion that the person is wealthy.

- As you read the story, think about how the three main characters act.

- Based on the characters' actions, what conclusions can you draw about them?

Folktale

"Jewel in the Sand" is a folktale that teaches a lesson about giving. As you read, think about how the characters act. What conclusions can you draw about them?

Jewel in the Sand

Adapted from *Arab Folktales,* edited by Inea Bushnaq

Sheik Hamid and his nephew Ali were riding their horses across the desert. The sheik was telling a long story. Suddenly, Ali saw something bright in the sand. Was it a jewel? He was **curious**, but he did not stop. It was not polite to **interrupt** his uncle's story.

Instead, Ali had an idea. On his back he carried a long sword. Ali put the point of the sword into the sand. It made a long line behind him as he rode home. Ali wanted to follow the line back to the jewel later.

Soon the two riders arrived at their camp. Friends welcomed them. The sheik went to his tent, but Ali turned his horse around. Quickly, he followed the line back through the sand. Was the jewel still there? Yes, it was. He picked it up. It was a beautiful green stone with gold around it. "This jewel must belong to a princess," Ali said.

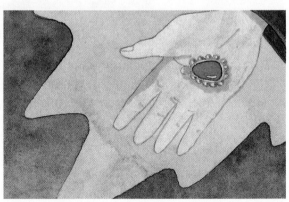

---

curious, wanting to know about something
interrupt, stop a person who is talking

MAKE CONNECTIONS

Did you ever find something special? Explain.

Ali returned and showed the jewel to his uncle. "The work on this jewel is very fine," said the sheik. "The owner of such a beautiful jewel must be a princess. We must find her." The sheik called an old woman to help him. He gave her the jewel. "Take this," he said. "Visit all the tribes around us. Find the person who lost this jewel."

The old woman went from camp to camp. No one knew who owned the jewel. Finally, she came to a big camp full of black tents. She entered a long tent. A beautiful young woman welcomed her. "Come in, Grandmother," she said.

The old woman sat for a while and rested. Then she opened the cloth that held the jewel. "Do you know who lost this jewel?" she asked. The girl's eyes opened wide. She ran to a wooden box. She took out a matching jewel.

"Here is my earring," said the young girl. "I lost the other one in the desert." She showed the old woman the two jewels in her hand. "Do you see how they match?"

The old woman saw that the jewels matched. "My child, take your jewel. But tell me your name and the name of your tribe."

The girl answered, "Grandmother, my name is not important. I want you to keep both jewels. You worked hard to find me. I give you the earrings as a gift."

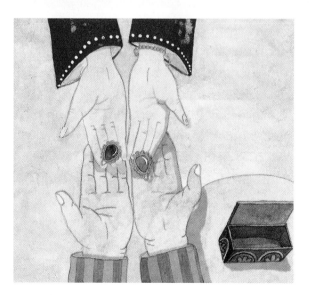

DISCUSS

1. Why do you think the princess called the old woman "Grandmother"?
2. How do you show respect for older people in your home country?

The old woman returned to her camp to tell the news to Sheik Hamid. He wanted to meet this princess. She was as **generous** as a king! He decided to ride to the camp of the black tents. He wanted to ask permission to marry the princess. The people there welcomed the sheik. The men brought food for his horses. The women cooked a big feast.

After three days, the sheik spoke to the prince, the father of the princess, "I rode here for a reason," said the sheik. "I came to ask to marry your daughter."

The prince looked sad. Then he said, "How can I refuse such a guest? My daughter and I bow our heads to you." The prince prepared marriage gifts to send with his daughter. "I give you seventy camels, many rugs, and many servants," he said. "My daughter will now be your bride. She is the jewel of the desert."

Soon the wedding day came. Sheik Hamid was walking to the wedding tent when a young man appeared. "Grant me the right to speak, Sheik Hamid!" he cried.

"You may speak without fear," said the sheik.

"The princess and I love each other. Her father knew this. But he could not refuse you because you were his guest. Please let me marry her!"

The sheik looked at the man. Then he said, "You ask only for what is fair. May you and your bride find joy."

So it is when people do what is right.

---

generous, giving

CHECK YOUR UNDERSTANDING

1 Why did the princess give the earrings to the old woman?

2 What kind of person is the princess?

3 Why does her father call her "the jewel of the desert"?

Jewel in the Sand ❖ A Play

Now read the same folktale as a play. There are eight parts.

CHARACTERS

Narrator	**Princess**
Ali	**Prince**
Sheik Hamid	**Young Man**
Old Woman	**Chorus**

Narrator: Sheik Hamid and his nephew Ali were riding their horses in the desert. The sheik was telling a story. Suddenly, Ali saw something bright in the sand.

Ali *(to himself)*: Is that a jewel?

Narrator: Ali did not stop to look. It was not polite to interrupt his uncle's story. But he lowered his sword into the sand to make a line behind him as he rode.

Chorus: Later that day, Ali followed the line back to the jewel.

Ali *(to himself)*: There it is! What a fine jewel.

Chorus: Ali returned and showed the jewel to his uncle.

Sheik Hamid: The owner of such a beautiful jewel must be a princess. We must find her. *(to the old woman)* Grandmother! We need your help! *(He gives the old woman the jewel.)* Find the person who lost this jewel.

Old Woman: Yes, Sheik Hamid.

Narrator: The old woman went from camp to camp. No one knew who owned the jewel. Finally, she came to a camp with big black tents. A beautiful princess welcomed her.

Princess: Come in, Grandmother. How can I help you?

Old Woman *(holding out the jewel):* Do you know who lost this?

Princess *(taking something out of a box):* Look, here is my earring. I lost its mate in the desert. See how they match!

Old Woman *(nodding):* Yes. Take back your jewel. But please tell me your name.

Princess: My name is not important. Here, I give you the two jewels as a gift.

Chorus: The old woman returned to her camp. She showed the sheik the jewels.

Sheik Hamid: I must meet this princess. She is as generous as a king.

Chorus: He rode to the camp with the black tents. There, he met the prince, the father of the princess.

Sheik Hamid: Good Prince, I came here to ask to marry your daughter.

Prince *(sadly):* How can I refuse such a guest? My daughter will be your bride. She is the jewel of the desert.

Narrator: Soon the wedding day came. The sheik was near the wedding tent when a young man spoke to him.

Young Man: The princess and I love each other. Her father knew this. But he could not refuse you because you were his guest. Please let me marry her!

Sheik Hamid: You ask only for what is fair. May you and your bride find joy.

Chorus: So it is when people do what is right.

Review and Practice

1. Look back at the pictures in "Jewel in the Sand" on pages 46–48. Cover the words on each page. Retell the events of the story to a partner, using only the pictures.

2. What conclusions did you draw about Ali, Sheik Hamid, and the princess? What kind of person was Ali? The sheik? The princess? How do you know?

COMPREHENSION

Write the sentences below in your notebook. Write *Yes* if statement is true. Write *No* if it is not true. Then rewrite the statement correctly. Reread pages 46–48 to check your answers.

1. Sheik Hamid and Ali were riding camels across the desert. *No.*
   Sheik Hamid and Ali were riding horses across the desert.
2. Ali saw something bright in the sand.
3. He put the point of a stick into the sand.
4. The sheik went to his yurt.
5. Ali returned and showed the jewel to his grandfather.
6. The sheik called an old woman to help him.
7. The princess gave the jewels to the sheik.
8. The prince prepared birthday gifts to send back with the sheik.

Extension

BIRTHSTONES

Birthstones are special jewels. There is a birthstone for each month. For example, the birthstone for January is a garnet. Look at the birthstones chart.

A. Talk about birthstones in small groups.

1. What is your birthstone?
2. What color is it?
3. Does anyone in your group have the same birthstone as you?
4. Which birthstone do you like the most? Why?

B. Make a poster about your birthstone. Follow the steps below:

1. Use the Interent or library books to find more information about your birthstone.
2. Paste or draw a picture of it in the middle of your poster. Write its name below the picture.
3. Write some facts about your birthstone around the picture. For example, tell what month your birthstone goes with. Tell what color it is, where it comes from, and what people make with it. You might also tell other interesting facts about it.
4. Draw lines from each fact to the picture of your birthstone.
5. Work with a partner. Tell each other about your birthstones.

BIRTHSTONES

JANUARY	FEBRUARY	MARCH
Garnet	Amethyst	Aquamarine
APRIL	MAY	JUNE
Diamond	Emerald	Pearl
JULY	AUGUST	SEPTEMBER
Ruby	Peridot	Sapphire
OCTOBER	NOVEMBER	DECEMBER
Opal	Topaz	Turquoise

Garnet is the birthstone for January.

Garnet

Some travelers carry garnets to protect themselves from accidents.

Connect to Writing

GRAMMAR

Articles

Articles are words that identify nouns. Nouns are the names of persons, places, or things. Use *a* or *an* to talk about one general person, place, or thing. Use *a* or *an* before singular nouns you can count.

> **A** princess lost **an** earring. (One princess lost one earring.)

• Use *a* before a consonant sound.

> He saw **a** jewel. They sleep in **a** tent.

• Use *an* before a vowel sound.

> Ali has **an** uncle. He had **an** idea.

• Do not use *a* or *an* before nouns you cannot count.

> I eat **rice** for dinner. We drink **coffee** in the morning.

• Use *the* to talk about one or more specific persons, places, or things.

> **The** Inuit were nomads. (The Inuit are specific people.)
> Ali found **the** earring. (Ali found the specific earring that the princess lost.)

• Do not use *a, an,* or *the* before names of places, months, days, or languages.

> My friends in **Canada** can speak **English** and **French.**
> I visited them in **July.**

Practice

Write these sentences in your notebook. Underline the article(s).

1. The Sioux hunted buffalo on the plains.
2. A sheik is a Bedouin leader.
3. The Mongolian nomads are an Asian people.
4. The sheik asked an old woman to find the owner of the earring.
5. The Inuit used boats called kayaks.
6. Many clans together make a tribe.

▲ Bedouin bags for coffee beans

52

SKILLS FOR WRITING

Writing a Journal Entry

People write in journals to record their thoughts and feelings about things that happen in their lives. Each separate writing in a journal is called an entry. A journal entry is personal and informal. *You* choose what to write about. You don't always need to write in complete sentences because you are writing for yourself. Writing journal entries can help you remember important events. It can also help you express your ideas and feelings more easily.

Imagine that the princess in "Jewel in the Sand" had a journal. Read the following entry. Then answer the questions.

> Monday
>
> What a terrible day! My father and I went to visit another camp. We were riding our horses in the desert, and it was windy. I reached up to get my hair out of my face. When my hand brushed past my ear, I didn't feel my earring. It was gone! I couldn't believe it. I felt my ear again. No earring. It must have fallen in the sand. How will I ever find it? What am I going to tell my father? Those earrings were his grandmother's! He will be so angry with me.

1. How was the princess feeling when she wrote this entry? How do you know?
2. How is her entry personal?
3. How is her entry informal?

WRITING PRACTICE

Journal Entry

Write a journal entry about something special you lost, a fun trip you took, or a gift someone gave you.

1. **Read** Reread the journal entry on page 53. What was special about the earring that the princess lost?

Writing Strategy: Freewriting

Journal entries are a kind of freewriting. When you freewrite, you write down thoughts and feelings quickly. A good way to freewrite is to time yourself. Set a timer for five minutes and start writing. Don't stop until the time is up. Don't think about grammar or punctuation. Write as many ideas as you can.

In the entry below, the writer is freewriting about a trip she took last summer.

> I took a trip with my family to San Francisco last summer. It was so much fun! We rode the cable cars up and down the many big hills. We ate lunch by San Francisco Bay and saw some seagulls. In the evening we ate dinner in Chinatown. The next day we visited Golden Gate Park and went to the Golden Gate Bridge. I bought a really cool model of the Golden Gate Bridge. My sister and brother got one too. What a great city—I want to go back there!

2. **Freewrite your journal entry** Think about something special you lost, a fun trip you took, or a gift that means a lot to you. Once you have an idea, take out a sheet of paper. Set a timer for five minutes and write without stopping. Write everything you remember about the idea or experience. Make sure you include your feelings.

Link the Readings

Make a chart like the one below to compare the readings in this unit. Look at each word in the column. Put an **X** under "Nomads" if the word reminds you of that selection. Put an **X** under "Jewel in the Sand" if the word reminds you of the folktale. Put an **X** in both places if the word reminds you of both selections.

	"Nomads"	"Jewel in the Sand"
fiction	_____	_____X_____
nonfiction	_____	_____
desert	_____	_____
tribe	_____	_____
sheik	_____	_____
buffalo	_____	_____
tents	_____	_____
Mongolia	_____	_____

Check Your Knowledge

Language Development
1. Do you think the people in "Jewel in the Sand" are Bedouins? Explain.
2. Name the three articles you learned about in this unit. Use each one in a sentence.
3. Give an example of drawing a conclusion. Use "Jewel in the Sand," another text, or your own experience.

Academic Content
1. Why do nomads travel from place to place?
2. Who are the Bedouins? Describe their way of life.
3. Why are animals important to nomads? Give examples.
4. How did the Sioux of North America use the buffalo that they hunted?

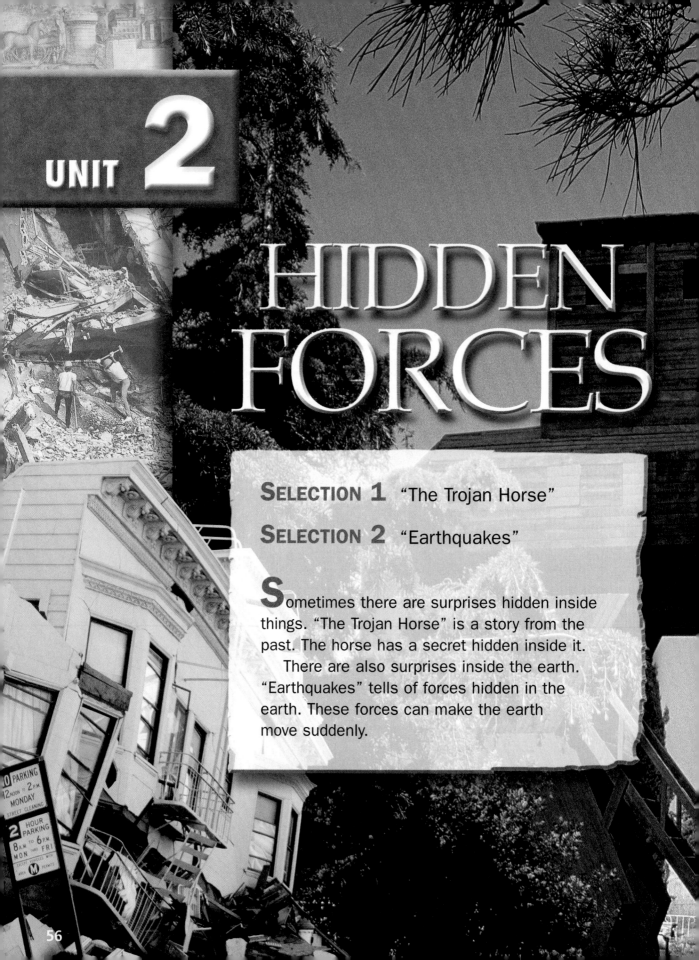

UNIT 2

HIDDEN FORCES

SELECTION 1 "The Trojan Horse"

SELECTION 2 "Earthquakes"

Sometimes there are surprises hidden inside things. "The Trojan Horse" is a story from the past. The horse has a secret hidden inside it.

There are also surprises inside the earth. "Earthquakes" tells of forces hidden in the earth. These forces can make the earth move suddenly.

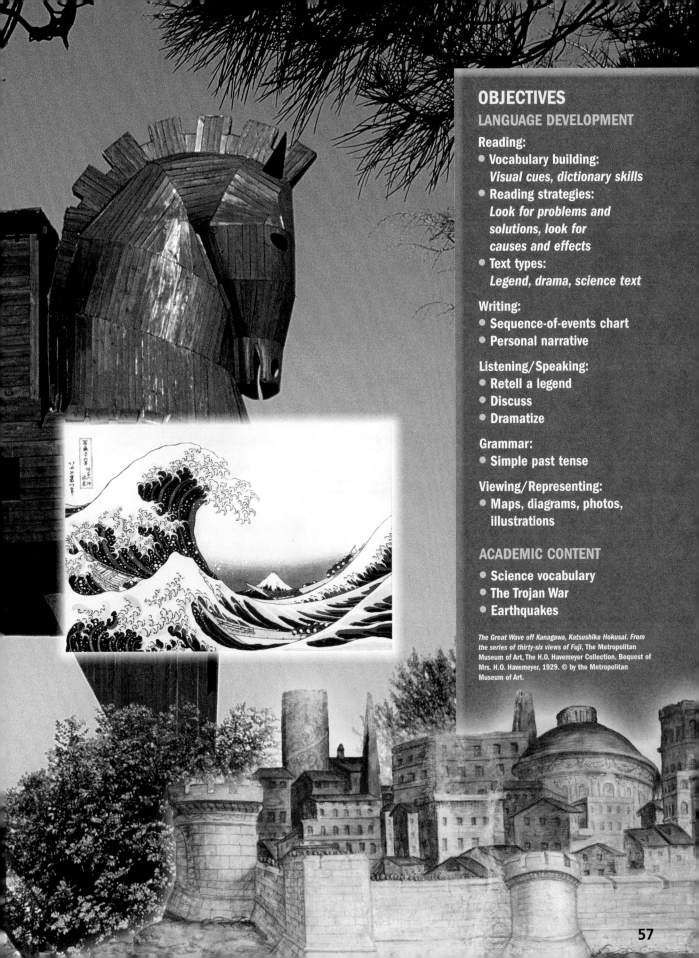

OBJECTIVES
LANGUAGE DEVELOPMENT

Reading:
- **Vocabulary building:**
  Visual cues, dictionary skills
- **Reading strategies:**
  Look for problems and solutions, look for causes and effects
- **Text types:**
  Legend, drama, science text

Writing:
- **Sequence-of-events chart**
- **Personal narrative**

Listening/Speaking:
- **Retell a legend**
- **Discuss**
- **Dramatize**

Grammar:
- **Simple past tense**

Viewing/Representing:
- **Maps, diagrams, photos, illustrations**

ACADEMIC CONTENT

- **Science vocabulary**
- **The Trojan War**
- **Earthquakes**

The Great Wave off Kanagawa, Katsushika Hokusai. From the series of thirty-six views of Fuji, The Metropolitan Museum of Art, The H.O. Havemeyer Collection. Bequest of Mrs. H.O. Havemeyer, 1929. © by the Metropolitan Museum of Art.

Prepare to Read

"The Trojan Horse" is a Greek legend. A legend is a story that people tell and retell over many, many years. Legends often change over time.

BLACK SEA

GREECE

AEGEAN SEA

Troy

TURKEY

MEDITERRANEAN SEA

▲ The Trojans lived in the ancient, or very old, city of Troy. Troy is marked with a star.

USE WHAT YOU KNOW

1. How do you think the Greeks traveled to Troy? Look at the map.

2. How do you think a big wooden horse could help an army?

▲ Model of the Trojan Horse at the site of ancient Troy in Turkey.

attack

enemies

palace

prisoner

soldiers

strong

VOCABULARY

Look at the pictures and the captions. They will help you learn the words in the box. Write the meaning of each word. Then check your work in a dictionary.

▲ Queen Helen was a **prisoner** inside the **palace** at Troy.

▲ The **strong** walls around Troy made the city safe.

◀ These Greek **soldiers** were ready to **attack** their **enemies,** the Trojans.

READING STRATEGY

Look for Problems and Solutions

In this legend, the Greeks had a **problem**. They needed to solve it, or find a **solution**. Read the story to find out what the problem was and how the Greeks solved it. Ask yourself these questions:

- What did the Greeks want to do?

- Why couldn't they do it?

- How did they solve their problem?

Legend

"The Trojan Horse" is a Greek legend based on history. Parts of the story really happened. Read it to find out how the Greeks solved their problem with the Trojans.

THE TROJAN HORSE

Helen was queen of the Greeks. She was very beautiful. A Trojan prince made her a prisoner and took her to his home in Troy. Helen's husband wanted Helen back in Greece. He sailed to Troy with many ships and many soldiers. For ten years he and the other Greeks **camped** outside the walls around the city. They attacked Troy many times, but the walls were too strong.

Finally, the Greeks asked two of their gods, Athena (uh-THEE-nuh) and Poseidon (po-SI-dun), for help. Athena wanted the Greeks to beat their enemies. She gave an idea to Odysseus (oh-DISS-ee-yus), one of the Greeks. Odysseus said, "We can trick the Trojans! We can build a huge wooden horse and hide inside it. Then, as soon as the Trojans bring the horse through the city walls, we will surprise them."

camped, lived in tents

CHECK YOUR UNDERSTANDING

Who gave Odysseus the idea to build a horse?

And that is what the Greek soldiers did. When the wooden horse was ready, they carved words on the side. The words said: *For Athena. The Greeks ask you for a safe return home.* The Greeks knew that the people of Troy also **honored** Athena. They knew there was a **temple** to Athena inside the city walls. This was their plan: "The Trojans will take the horse into the city to the temple. We will be hiding inside the horse."

That night, Odysseus and twenty other soldiers climbed inside the horse. They closed the small door and waited quietly. All the other Greeks sailed away in their ships, but they did not go far.

The next morning, the Trojans looked outside the walls. The Greeks were gone. Their camp was empty. Nothing was left outside the walls of Troy but the big wooden horse.

The Trojans saw the huge horse and were curious about it. One Trojan warned that the horse was a trick. But the others did not listen. They decided to bring it through the city walls. It was very heavy. With great effort, they pulled it into the city. When the horse was inside, the people of Troy covered it with flowers.

---

honored, treated as special; respected
temple, place where people worship in some religions

CHECK YOUR UNDERSTANDING

Why did the Greeks think the Trojans would take the horse into the city?

At night the king of Troy had a party at the palace. At last the war was over. Queen Helen came outside to look at the horse. "I wonder what is inside this horse," she said quietly to herself. The men inside the horse wanted to call out to Helen, but Odysseus stopped them.

"Shhh," he said to his men. "Do not say a word or the Trojans will **discover** us." Helen guessed that Greek soldiers were inside the horse, but she kept the secret.

Late that night, all the Trojans were asleep. The Greek soldiers opened the small door in the horse. They climbed out. A few of them ran to the top of the city walls. They waved at their ships to return. The Greek soldiers on the ships saw them and sailed back to the city.

Then Odysseus and his men opened the city gates. All the other Greek soldiers rushed inside. They killed the Trojans and burned the city. Queen Helen was saved. The long war was over.

---

discover, find

CHECK YOUR UNDERSTANDING

How did the horse help the Greeks win the war?

THE TROJAN HORSE ✳ A Play

Now read the same legend as a play. There are twelve parts.

CHARACTERS

Narrator	First Trojan Soldier
Helen's Husband	Second Trojan Soldier
Athena	Trojan Man
Odysseus	Trojan King
First Greek Soldier	Queen Helen
Second Greek Soldier	Chorus

Narrator: Helen, queen of the Greeks, was a prisoner in Troy. Her husband wanted her back in Greece.

Helen's Husband (to soldiers)**:** We must get Helen out of Troy!

Narrator: The Greeks sailed to Troy. They attacked the city for ten years. But the walls around Troy were very strong.

Chorus: The Greeks called to the gods for help. Athena! Poseidon!

Athena: I will help my people win. I will give an idea to Odysseus.

Odysseus: I have an idea! We can trick the Trojans. We can build a huge horse and hide inside it.

First Greek Soldier: We'll carve these words on it: *For Athena. The Greeks ask you for a safe return home.*

Odysseus: The Trojans will think the horse is for Athena. They honor her just as we do.

Second Greek Soldier: The Trojans will bring the horse inside their city. Then we will surprise them.

Narrator: The Greek soldiers built the huge horse. When it was ready, Odysseus and twenty other soldiers climbed inside.

Odysseus: Close the door! Be quiet!

Chorus: The Greeks' ships left Troy, but they did not go far.

First Trojan Soldier: Look! What did the Greeks leave behind?

Second Trojan Soldier: It is a gift for Athena. Call the others. We can take it into the city.

Trojan Man: No! Wait. It must be a trick.

Chorus: Don't listen to him!

First Trojan Soldier: Open the gates! We have a gift for Athena.

Narrator: The Trojans pulled the horse into the city.

Trojan King: The war is over. Now we will have a feast at the palace.

Queen Helen (to herself, looking at the horse)**:** What is inside this horse?

Odysseus (quietly, to the other men inside the horse)**:** Shhh! Don't say a word!

Narrator: The Greek soldiers came out of the horse. The people of Troy were asleep.

First Greek Soldier: I will climb the walls and wave at the ships.

Second Greek Soldier: I will open the gates.

All the Greek Soldiers: Now, soldiers! Attack! Burn the city!

Chorus: So the Greeks won the war, and Helen was saved.

Review and Practice

RETELL AND REVIEW

1. Look back at the pictures in "The Trojan Horse" on pages 60–62. Cover the words on each page. Retell the events of the story to a partner, using only the pictures.
2. What problem did the Greeks have to solve?
3. How did the Greeks solve their problem?

COMPREHENSION

Complete the sentences. Choose the correct word from the column on the right. Write the completed sentences in your notebook.

1. The walls around Troy were very _strong_.
2. Helen was a _____ in Troy.
3. Athena gave an idea to _____.
4. The Trojans thought the horse was a gift for _____.
5. All the other Greeks sailed away in their _____.
6. The Trojans pulled the horse through the city _____.
7. The Trojan king had a feast at the _____.
8. Late at night, all the Trojans were _____.
9. The Greek soldiers on the ships _____.
10. The Greeks _____ Helen and won the war.

Odysseus

~~strong~~

Athena

returned

prisoner

saved

asleep

palace

ships

gates

Extension

GREEK GODS

A. Read about Poseidon. He was one of many Greek gods.

Poseidon was the god of the sea. The Greeks asked Poseidon for help in fighting against the Trojans. The Greeks believed Poseidon could make storms in the sea. They also believed he could shake the earth, making walls and buildings fall. Poseidon was also the god of horses. Some people think that the Trojan horse really stood for Poseidon. They think that the walls around Troy fell because Poseidon made the earth shake.

B. Find out more about Poseidon or another Greek god. Follow these steps:

1. Read library books or use the Internet.
2. Choose a Greek god to write about.
3. Write a paragraph. Answer these questions:
   - What does the god look like?
   - What does the god do?
   - What powers does the god have?
4. Read your paragraph to the class.

Prepare to Read

"Earthquakes" is nonfiction. It is like the text you find in science books. It tells how and why earthquakes happen.

Earthquakes can cause great damage, or harm. Some people think that an earthquake caused the walls of Troy to fall. Troy was in a part of the world where many earthquakes have happened. Why do earthquakes happen more often in some places than in others? Read "Earthquakes" to find out.

▲ An earthquake in 1989 damaged this house in San Francisco, California.

USE WHAT YOU KNOW

1. Have you ever felt an earthquake? Explain.
2. Do you think all earthquakes cause damage? Why or why not?

LEARN KEY WORDS

crust
dangerous
destroy
directions
plates
powerful

VOCABULARY

Look at the pictures and the captions. They will help you learn the words in the box. Write the meaning of each word. Then check your work in a dictionary.

▲ A **powerful** earthquake can **destroy** buildings.

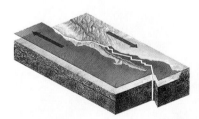

◀ These are **plates,** pieces of the earth's **crust.** They are moving in different **directions**.

▲ Living in places where earthquakes happen can be **dangerous**.

READING STRATEGY
Look for Causes and Effects

"Earthquakes" tells why earthquakes happen. Why something happens is a **cause**. What happens is an **effect**. Writers often use the words *cause* and *causes* to show cause and effect.

- Read to find out why earthquakes happen.
- Look for the words *cause* and *causes*.
- Read to find out some effects of earthquakes.

"Earthquakes" is nonfiction text that tells where and how earthquakes happen. Read the selection to learn about the causes and effects of earthquakes.

EARTHQUAKES

What Is an Earthquake?

An earthquake is a sudden moving or shaking of the ground. *Quake* is another word for *shake*. Earthquakes can be mild or very powerful. Powerful earthquakes can destroy buildings and bridges. They can also cause rivers to change direction. Earthquakes under the ocean can cause

CHECK YOUR UNDERSTANDING

What kinds of damage can earthquakes cause?

▲ A powerful earthquake in 1985 destroyed many buildings in Mexico City.

huge waves, called tsunamis (soo-NAH-meez), to crash onto the land. Few earthquakes last more than thirty seconds.

What Is the Earth's Crust?

The earth's crust is a layer of rock that covers the earth. It is underneath all the land and water on the earth. The crust is made of huge pieces of rock called plates. The plates move very slowly. Where the plates touch, they can push against each other. These areas are called faults.

What Happens along the Faults?

Along the faults, the rocks press together. The **pressure** builds up between the plates until one of the plates snaps past the other. This causes the rock along the faults to shake. The shaking is an earthquake. During an earthquake, the earth's crust can crack. These huge cracks usually happen along the faults.

---

pressure, force created by pressing

▲ An underwater earthquake in 1993 caused a tsunami that crashed onto Okushiri Island in Japan. It destroyed everything in its path.

▲ The earth's crust is made up of plates.

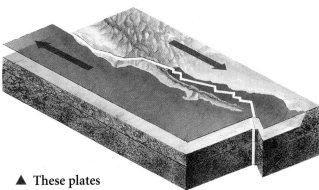

▲ These plates are moving in opposite directions. This causes pressure to build up where the plates touch. In time, the plates will snap past each other, causing an earthquake.

CHECK YOUR UNDERSTANDING

1 What are plates?

2 What happens when pressure builds up between plates?

Where Do Earthquakes Happen?

Most earthquakes happen along the faults, where the plates meet. Look at the map. It shows the plates in the earth's crust. One of the places where earthquakes happen is Turkey, where the city of Troy once was. Other places where earthquakes happen include Mexico, Japan, and California. As you can see, earthquakes can happen all over the world!

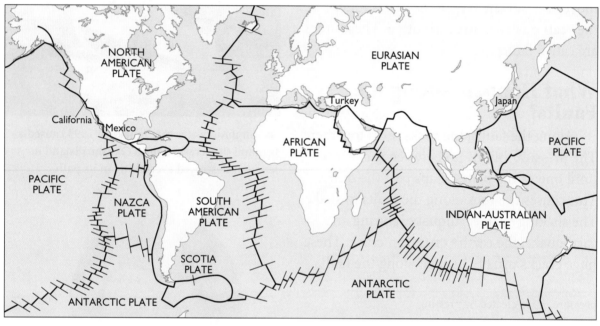

▲ This map shows the plates in the earth's crust. Most earthquakes happen where the plates meet.

◀ An earthquake in 1999 hit the city of Golcuk, in Turkey. Golcuk is right on a fault line. The ancient city of Troy, also in Turkey, was on a fault line, too.

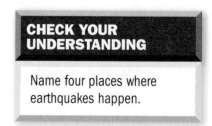

CHECK YOUR UNDERSTANDING

Name four places where earthquakes happen.

70

What Is the San Andreas Fault?

The San Andreas Fault in California is famous. It is where the Pacific plate slides against the North American plate. Earthquakes along this fault usually happen closer to the earth's surface than at other places. They cause more shaking. These types of earthquakes are more dangerous than ones deep under the ground.

How Do We Measure Earthquakes?

We measure earthquakes by using a special machine called a seismograph (SIZE-moh-graf). The word *seismograph* comes from the Greek word *seismos,* which means "earthquake." Earthquakes cause waves to pass through the earth's crust. Stronger earthquakes make bigger waves, and weaker earthquakes make smaller waves. A seismograph records the size of the waves and how far away the earthquake is.

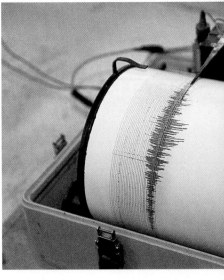

▲ A seismograph measures earthquakes by recording the force of the waves.

NORTH AMERICA

▲ San Andreas Fault in California

CHECK YOUR UNDERSTANDING

1 What two plates meet at the San Andreas Fault?

2 Why are earthquakes along the San Andreas Fault often dangerous?

71

Review and Practice

1. Tell a partner what you learned about earthquakes. Use the headings and the pictures on pages 68–71 to help you.

2. What causes and effects did you find when you read "Earthquakes"? List each cause and effect that you found.

COMPREHENSION

Write the sentences below in your notebook. Write *Yes* if the statement is true. Write *No* if it is not true. Then rewrite the statement correctly. Reread pages 68–71 to check your answers.

1. Earthquakes cannot change the direction of rivers. *No. Earthquakes can change the direction of rivers.*

2. Most earthquakes last for hours.

3. The earth's crust is made up of solid rock.

4. During an earthquake the earth's crust can crack.

5. Pressure in the earth's crust causes earthquakes.

6. Earthquakes can cause tsunamis.

7. Earthquakes deep under the ground cause more damage than earthquakes at the surface.

8. We measure earthquakes with thermometers.

Extension

MODELS

People use models to show what something is like. For example, a globe is a model of the earth. A globe has the same shape as the earth. It shows the earth's land and oceans.

You can make a model showing what happens when plates that make up the earth's crust push against each other. Follow the steps below.

You will need:
- modeling clay in three colors
- a rolling pin
- a strong plastic knife
- a small empty box (size of paper-clip box)

1. Put the three pieces of modeling clay on a table.
2. Roll each piece of clay into a slab 1 centimeter (½ in.) thick.
3. Cut each clay slab into a square measuring 16 x 16 centimeters (6 x 6 in.).
4. Place one square on top of the other, like a sandwich.
5. Cut the clay "sandwich" in half, making two rectangles, 8 x 16 centimeters (3 x 6 in.) each.
6. Turn the pieces so that the long, smooth sides are touching, side by side.
7. Balance a small empty box on one rectangle.
8. Push the rectangles in opposite directions. Keep them pressed against each other as they slowly move past each other.

What happened to the box? How is that like an earthquake?

73

Connect to Writing

GRAMMAR

The Simple Past Tense: Regular and Irregular Verbs

Use the **simple past tense** to talk about completed actions in the past. For most **regular** verbs, add *-ed* to the base form.

> The Greeks sail**ed** to Troy.
> The soldiers camp**ed** outside the walls.
> The earthquake happen**ed** in Mexico City.

When a regular verb ends in *-e*, add *-d*.

> The Greek soldiers close**d** the door.
> He use**d** a seismograph to measure the earthquake.

Many verbs have **irregular** past-tense forms. The chart gives some examples.

base form	simple past	base form	simple past
do	**did**	keep	**kept**
give	**gave**	know	**knew**
go	**went**	make	**made**
have	**had**	see	**saw**

Be is a special irregular verb. Use *was* with *I, he, she,* or *it*. Use *were* with *you, we,* and *they*.

> Odysseus **was** a Greek soldier.
> Athena and Poseidon **were** Greek gods.

Practice

Rewrite each sentence with a correct past-tense verb. Use the charts above.

1. Beautiful Helen __*was*__ queen of the Greeks. (be)

2. A Trojan prince _____ her a prisoner. (make)

3. The Trojans _____ the huge horse. (see)

4. At last the war _____ over. (be)

5. Queen Helen _____ that soldiers were inside the horse. (know)

SKILLS FOR WRITING

Writing a Personal Narrative

A narrative tells a story. A **personal narrative** tells a story about an experience you had. You usually tell a personal narrative in the order that the events happened.

You can use sequence words to show the order of events. Sequence words usually come at the beginning of a sentence. Some sequence words are *first, next, then, after that,* and *finally.*

Read about Zin's unusual experience. Then answer the questions.

Zin Dong

Our Shaky Day

Last Tuesday, my mother and I had breakfast as usual. But it wasn't usual for long. First, our glasses of orange juice shook. Then the table shook. After that, we watched our glasses slide. Crash! They fell off the table and broke on the floor. We knew it was an earthquake!

My mother felt really scared, but I remembered what to do. First, I helped her stand up. Then we stood in the doorway between the kitchen and the hall. A doorway is the safest place in an earthquake. Next, we breathed slowly to stay calm. Finally, the earthquake was over! It only lasted for about thirty seconds, but it seemed like thirty minutes.

---

1. What happened to Zin and her mother?
2. How do you know that this is a personal narrative?
3. What words show the order of events?

WRITING PRACTICE

Personal Narrative

You will write a personal narrative about an unusual experience you had.

1. Read Reread the personal narrative on page 75.

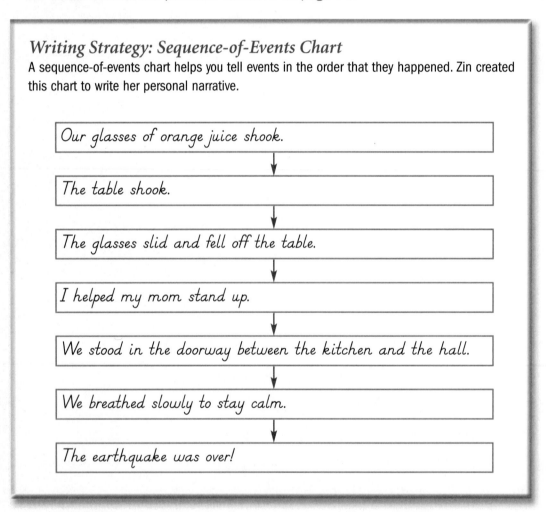

Writing Strategy: Sequence-of-Events Chart

A sequence-of-events chart helps you tell events in the order that they happened. Zin created this chart to write her personal narrative.

> Our glasses of orange juice shook.
>
> The table shook.
>
> The glasses slid and fell off the table.
>
> I helped my mom stand up.
>
> We stood in the doorway between the kitchen and the hall.
>
> We breathed slowly to stay calm.
>
> The earthquake was over!

2. Make a sequence-of-events chart Make a chart about your experience in your notebook. Write the events in the order that they happened.

3. Write Write a personal narrative. Use the events from your chart. Remember to use sequence words to show the order of events.

Link the Readings

Make a chart like the one below to compare the readings in this unit. Look at each word in the column. Put an **X** under "The Trojan Horse" if the word reminds you of the legend. Put an **X** under "Earthquakes" if the word reminds you of that selection. Put an **X** in both places if the word reminds you of both selections.

	"The Trojan Horse"	"Earthquakes"
legend	_____	_____
science text	_____	_____
Athena	_____	_____
Poseidon	_____	_____
plates	_____	_____
faults	_____	_____
hidden forces	_____	_____
Odysseus	_____	_____

Check Your Knowledge

Language Development
1. What is a legend? How is it different from a folktale? Explain and give an example.
2. How does thinking about problems and solutions help you as you read?
3. Give examples of verbs with regular and irregular past-tense forms.
4. What is a sequence-of-events chart? What does it show?

Academic Content
1. What was the Trojan Horse?
2. Name three places in the world where earthquakes have happened.
3. What do scientists think causes an earthquake?
4. How are earthquakes measured?

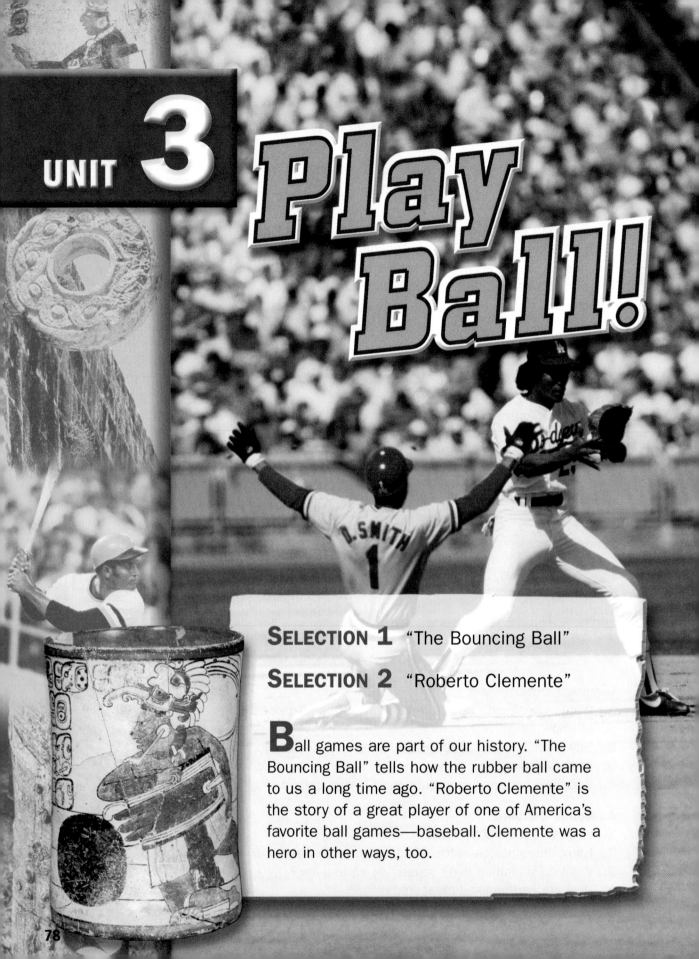

Play Ball!

SELECTION 1 "The Bouncing Ball"

SELECTION 2 "Roberto Clemente"

Ball games are part of our history. "The Bouncing Ball" tells how the rubber ball came to us a long time ago. "Roberto Clemente" is the story of a great player of one of America's favorite ball games—baseball. Clemente was a hero in other ways, too.

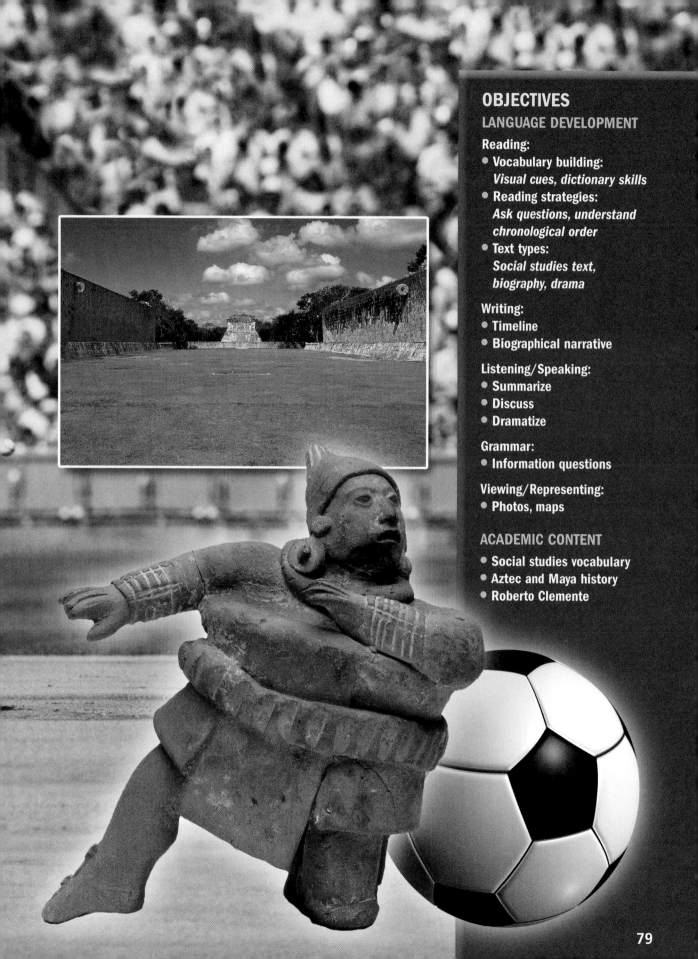

OBJECTIVES

LANGUAGE DEVELOPMENT

Reading:
- Vocabulary building:
  Visual cues, dictionary skills
- Reading strategies:
  *Ask questions, understand
  chronological order*
- Text types:
  *Social studies text,
  biography, drama*

Writing:
- Timeline
- Biographical narrative

Listening/Speaking:
- Summarize
- Discuss
- Dramatize

Grammar:
- Information questions

Viewing/Representing:
- Photos, maps

ACADEMIC CONTENT

- Social studies vocabulary
- Aztec and Maya history
- Roberto Clemente

79

Prepare to Read

"The Bouncing Ball" is nonfiction. It gives you facts about the history of the rubber ball.

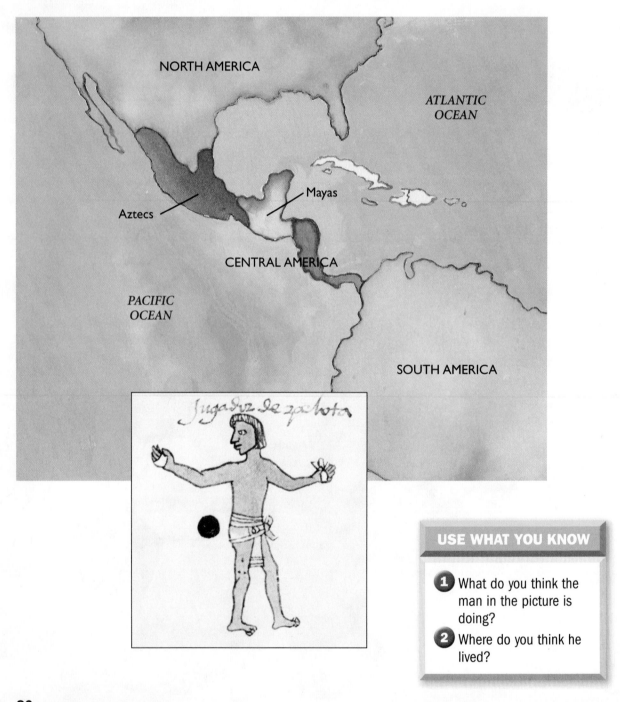

NORTH AMERICA

ATLANTIC OCEAN

Aztecs

Mayas

CENTRAL AMERICA

PACIFIC OCEAN

SOUTH AMERICA

USE WHAT YOU KNOW

1 What do you think the man in the picture is doing?

2 Where do you think he lived?

LEARN KEY WORDS

artifact
bounce
explorers
rubber
statue

VOCABULARY

Look at the pictures and the captions. They will help you learn the words in the box. Write the meaning of each word. Then check your work in a dictionary.

▲ **Rubber** comes from the liquid inside rubber trees. Most balls made of rubber can **bounce** up and down.

◄ This **statue** of a Maya ballplayer is an **artifact**. An artifact is an object made by people. We learn about ancient peoples from the artifacts they leave behind.

▲ Spanish **explorers** traveled to the Americas in the 1500s. There they met the Aztec (AZ-tek) and Maya (MY-uh) peoples.

READING STRATEGY

Ask Questions

Ask questions as you read to check what you know and don't know. For example, ask yourself, "What ideas or words don't I understand?"

- Write down words or ideas you don't understand.
- Reread the text and look for the meanings of these words or ideas.
- Use a dictionary or ask your teacher for help when necessary.

Social Studies

Nonfiction gives you facts about a subject. "The Bouncing Ball" tells about the ball games people played a long time ago. As you read, ask yourself questions about the text.

The Bouncing Ball

Where Did This New Ball Come From?

Most people in Europe did not know about rubber balls until the 1500s. Before that time, Europeans played games with balls made of wood or leather. They did not have balls that bounced. They did not play ball games like basketball, soccer, or tennis.

In the early 1500s, explorers from Spain went to what is now Mexico and Central America to look for gold. There the Spanish explorers met the Aztec and Maya peoples. The Aztecs and the Mayas played games with a new kind of ball. This ball bounced up and down. At first, the Spanish were afraid of this strange ball. What made it bounce? Was there something inside it? Did the Aztecs and Mayas have a secret?

▲ Maya ballplayer

▲ Players tried to bounce a rubber ball through a stone ring.

USE WHAT YOU KNOW

Why do you think the Spanish were afraid of the bouncing ball?

▲ Rubber tree

▲ An ancient
rubber ball

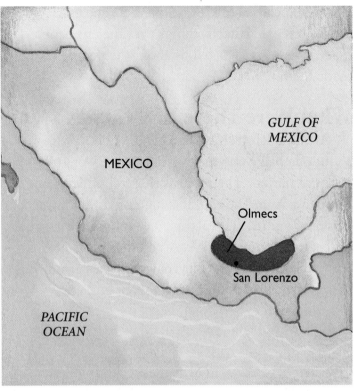

GULF OF
MEXICO

MEXICO

Olmecs

San Lorenzo

PACIFIC
OCEAN

▲ Ancient rubber balls were found in Olmec ruins near San Lorenzo, Mexico.

This strange ball was heavy. It was not made of wood or leather. It was made of rubber. The Aztecs and Mayas made rubber from the **sap** of rubber trees. The Spanish did not know about rubber trees. Rubber trees did not grow in Spain.

Who Were the Olmecs?

No one knows exactly when people first used rubber balls. Scientists think the Olmec people had rubber balls as early as 1000 B.C.E. The Olmecs lived in parts of what is now Mexico and Central America before the Aztecs and Mayas. Their name, *Olmec*, means "rubber people."

In 1989, scientists found three ancient rubber balls in Olmec **ruins** near San Lorenzo, Mexico. They also

> **MAKE CONNECTIONS**
>
> What parts of a car are made of rubber?

---

sap, liquid inside trees
ruins, remains of buildings where people lived long ago

discovered clay statues of ballplayers. The balls and the statues are artifacts, things that ancient people made. These artifacts tell us about the people who made them.

What Were These Ball Games Like?

Artifacts left by the Mayas and Aztecs tell us about one ball game they played. There were two teams of players. The players tried to bounce a ball through a ring. The ring was high on a wall in the center of a court. The players did not use their hands or feet to hit the ball. They used other parts of their bodies. Sometimes the players wore yokes around their waists or pads on their knees or elbows for protection.

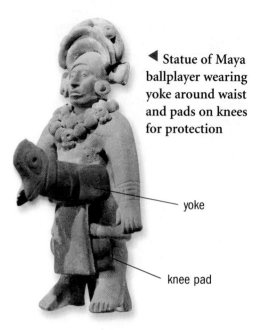

◄ Statue of Maya ballplayer wearing yoke around waist and pads on knees for protection

yoke

knee pad

▲ Ancient ball court in Mexico with stone rings high on walls

MAKE CONNECTIONS

1 Is the ball game that the Mayas and Aztecs played like any game you know? Explain.

2 Do you ever wear pads when you play a sport? Explain.

How Are Our Ball Games Like Theirs?

The Spanish explorers took Aztec and Maya ballplayers back to Europe in 1521. Europeans loved the new ball games. They began to use rubber balls themselves and made up new games. Later, when Europeans came to North America, they invented other ball games. Many of the sports we play today come from the early Aztec and Maya games in some way. Here are some examples:

- In most of our sports today, we use balls that bounce.
- We play ball games on ball courts or fields.
- Two teams play against each other.
- Sometimes the players wear pads to protect themselves.

When you play games with a bouncing ball, you are part of history. You are continuing games that began on ancient ball courts 3,000 years ago.

▲ Soccer players pass the ball without using their hands or arms. They wear pads to protect their legs.

▲ Volleyball is played on a court.

▲ Basketball players throw the ball through a hoop at the end of a court.

MAKE CONNECTIONS

1. What is your favorite sport? Why do you like it?
2. Does that sport use a bouncing ball? Explain.

85

Review and Practice

1. Tell a partner what you learned about Aztec and Maya ball games. Use the headings and the pictures on pages 82–85 to help you.

2. What questions did you ask yourself as you read "The Bouncing Ball"? How did you answer these questions?

COMPREHENSION

Write the questions below in your notebook. Then write an answer after each question. Use complete sentences.

1. Why did Spanish explorers go to the Americas in the early 1500s?
   Spanish explorers went to the Americas to look for gold.

2. What did the Spanish think of the rubber ball when they first saw it?

3. What is an artifact? What do artifacts tell us?

4. What kinds of balls did Europeans use in their games before the 1500s?

5. What is rubber made from?

6. How did the Aztecs and Mayas play their ball games?

7. How did the rubber ball get to Europe?

8. List three ways in which Aztec and Maya ball games are like our sports.

Extension

ARTIFACTS

Why Are Artifacts Important?

Artifacts tell us how people from a different time lived. They answer questions like these:

- Where did the people live?
- What did these people wear?
- What did they eat?
- What games did they play?

A. Work in a small group. Look at the pictures. Discuss what each object tells about how people live today.

B. Pretend that it is the year 4010. A scientist finds the ruins of your house. There are many artifacts there. Which artifacts tell the scientist the most about how you lived?

1. Make a list of artifacts that the scientist might find. Choose artifacts that would give answers to the questions at the top of the page.

2. Make a chart. In the left column, copy your list of artifacts. In the right column, explain what each artifact tells about how you lived.

Artifact	What It Tells
Cell phone	People had to talk to each other a lot.

3. Paste the chart onto a sheet of paper. Then add photos or drawings of the artifacts.

4. Share your work with the class.

Prepare to Read

"Roberto Clemente" is a biography. A biography is the true story of a person's life. It is written by someone else. A biography is nonfiction because the people and events in it are real.

▲ Roberto Clemente was born in Puerto Rico. He became a great baseball player.

USE WHAT YOU KNOW

1. What do you know about baseball? Tell a partner some things you like and dislike about it.

2. Find Puerto Rico on the map below. Share some things you know about Puerto Rico with your classmates.

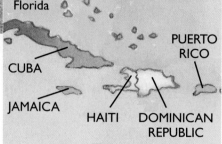

Florida

CUBA

JAMAICA

HAITI

DOMINICAN REPUBLIC

PUERTO RICO

LEARN KEY WORDS

achievements
medicine
opportunity
rescue
supplies

VOCABULARY

Look at the pictures and the captions. They will help you learn the words in the box. Write the meaning of each word. Then check your work in a dictionary.

▲ One of Roberto Clemente's greatest **achievements** was being voted Most Valuable Player of the National League in 1966.

◀ The Pittsburgh Pirates gave Roberto Clemente the **opportunity** to play baseball.

◀ **Rescue** workers bring **medicine** and other **supplies** to people in need.

READING STRATEGY

Understand Chronological Order

A biography tells events in **chronological**, or time, **order**. Writers use time phrases such as *in 1934, on May 30,* and *the next year* to tell you when events happen.

- As you read, look for time phrases and important events.
- Make a T-chart to help you remember the dates and events. On the left side, write the dates. On the right side, write the events.

Biography

"Roberto Clemente" is a biography. It is the true story of Roberto Clemente's life. The people and events in it are real. As you read, look for time phrases that tell when events happened.

ROBERTO CLEMENTE

Roberto Clemente was born in Carolina, Puerto Rico, in 1934. His father worked on a sugar cane **plantation**, and his mother worked in a grocery store. As a boy, Roberto loved baseball. His family didn't have much money, so Roberto had to make his own baseballs. He took old golf balls and wrapped string and tape around them to make them the right size.

Roberto played baseball in high school. After high school, he played for a team in Puerto Rico. In 1953, the Brooklyn Dodgers asked Roberto to join one of their **minor league** teams in Montreal, Canada. The next year, the Pittsburgh Pirates chose him to play for them in the **major leagues**. Roberto moved to Pittsburgh, Pennsylvania, and played **right field** for the Pirates for the next eighteen years. He became one of the best players in the major leagues.

---

plantation, large farm
minor league, less important group of teams of baseball players
major leagues, most important groups of teams of baseball players
right field, position in a baseball field

USE WHAT YOU KNOW

What do you think Roberto Clemente's childhood was like? Explain.

His fans called him "The Great One." Roberto didn't speak English well, so reporters and sports writers sometimes **made fun of** him. Roberto didn't listen to them. He played great baseball and helped other Spanish-speaking players.

In 1971, the Pirates played against the Baltimore Orioles in the World Series, the games that decide the best baseball team in North America. Roberto was amazing! In seven games, he had 12 hits, including 2 **home runs**, 2 **doubles**, and 1 **triple**. The Pirates won the Series, and Roberto was voted Most Valuable Player of the Series.

Another of Roberto's great achievements happened on September 30, 1972. He got his three-thousandth hit as a major league player. At that time, he was only the eleventh player ever to get that many hits. But the hit was to be his last.

▲ Roberto with his wife and son and the trophy for Most Valuable Player of the National League in 1966

---

made fun of, laughed at, said unkind things about
home runs, hits that let the batter run around all the bases and score a run
doubles, hits that get the batter to second base
triple, hit that gets the batter to third base

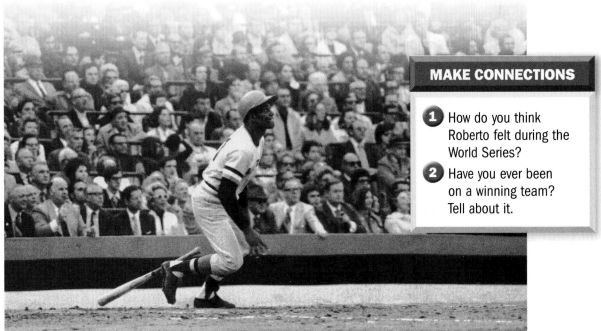

▲ Clemente batting in the World Series, 1971

MAKE CONNECTIONS

1. How do you think Roberto felt during the World Series?
2. Have you ever been on a winning team? Tell about it.

▲ "The Great One"

ROBERTO CLEMENTE WALKER
PITTSBURGH N. L. 1955-1972

MEMBER OF EXCLUSIVE 3,000-HIT CLUB. LED NATIONAL LEAGUE IN BATTING FOUR TIMES. HAD FOUR SEASONS WITH 200 OR MORE HITS WHILE POSTING LIFETIME .317 AVERAGE AND 240 HOME RUNS. WON MOST VALUABLE PLAYER AWARD 1966. RIFLE-ARMED DEFENSIVE STAR SET N. L. MARK BY PACING OUTFIELDERS IN ASSISTS FIVE YEARS. BATTED .362 IN TWO WORLD SERIES, HITTING IN ALL 14 GAMES.

▲ Roberto Clemente was elected to the Baseball Hall of Fame.

On December 23, 1972, three earthquakes hit the city of Managua, Nicaragua. More than 10,000 people died, and more than 250,000 people lost their homes. Most of the buildings in the city were destroyed. The city had no water, electricity, or gas. Rescue workers there needed help.

Roberto had once said, "Anytime you have an opportunity to make things better and you don't, you are wasting your time on this earth." Roberto now had a chance to help the people of Nicaragua. On New Year's Eve, he and four friends loaded a plane with medicine and other supplies and took off from Puerto Rico to Nicaragua. But they never got there. The plane crashed into the ocean, and Roberto and his friends died.

After he died, people honored Roberto in many ways. Sports writers **elected** him to the **Baseball Hall of Fame** in 1973. He was the first player from Latin America ever to receive this honor. People all over the world named schools and hospitals after him. And his wife and sons collected money to build a sports center for children in Puerto Rico. It was something Roberto had always planned to do.

---

elected, chose
Baseball Hall of Fame, museum in New York State that honors people important to baseball

MAKE CONNECTIONS

1. Today, players on U.S. sports teams come from many different countries. Name a few of these players.

2. Why do you think so many people loved Roberto Clemente?

Roberto Clemente ⚾ A Play

Now read the same story as a play. There are eight parts.

CHARACTERS

Narrator
Roberto's Mother
Roberto
Sports Writer 1

Sports Writer 2
Fans
Reporter
Chorus

Narrator: Roberto Clemente was born in Carolina, Puerto Rico, in 1934. His father worked on a sugar cane plantation, and his mother worked in a grocery store.

Roberto's Mother: Roberto loved baseball. As a boy, he played baseball whenever he could. We didn't have much money, so we couldn't buy baseballs for him. He used to make baseballs out of old golf balls.

Narrator: In 1953, Roberto got great news.

Roberto's Mother *(proudly):* The Brooklyn Dodgers asked Roberto to play for one of their minor league teams in Canada!

Narrator: The next year, Roberto received better news.

Roberto: The Pittsburgh Pirates have chosen me to play in the major leagues!

Sports Writer 1: Roberto Clemente can do it all. He can run, hit, catch, and throw.

Sports Writer 2: He doesn't talk to reporters much. His English isn't very good.

Roberto: It is hard for Spanish-speaking players to play baseball in the United States. I must do all I can to help them.

Fans: Roberto, you are a great ballplayer *and* a great person. You are "The Great One"! We love you!

Narrator: In 1971, the Pirates beat the Baltimore Orioles in the World Series.

Sports Writer 1: Roberto Clemente was voted Most Valuable Player of the Series.

Narrator: A year later, Roberto got his three-thousandth hit as a major league player.

Roberto's Mother *(sadly):* That was Roberto's very last hit.

Reporter: On December 23, 1972, three earthquakes hit Managua, Nicaragua.

Chorus: Thousands of people died. Thousands of others lost their homes.

Roberto: Anytime you have an opportunity to make things better and you don't, you are wasting your time on this earth. I must help the people of Nicaragua.

Narrator: Roberto and four friends tried to fly to Nicaragua from Puerto Rico.

Chorus: Their plane crashed on New Year's Eve and Roberto and his friends died.

Sports Writer 1: Today, we honor Roberto Clemente by electing him to the Baseball Hall of Fame.

Chorus: People all over the world named schools and hospitals after him.

Roberto's Mother: Roberto's family built a sports center for the children of Puerto Rico.

Chorus: It's what The Great One always wanted to do.

Review and Practice

1. Tell a partner what you learned about Roberto Clemente. Use the pictures and the captions on pages 90–92 to help you.

2. How did your T-chart of events help you to understand the biography better? Work with a partner to compare the events you listed.

COMPREHENSION

Complete the sentences. Choose the correct answer from the column on the right. Write the completed sentences in your notebook.

1. Roberto Clemente was born in _Puerto Rico_.   Nicaragua

2. Roberto made his own baseballs from old _____.   English

3. Roberto did not speak _____ very well.   home runs

4. Roberto hit two _____ during the 1971 World Series.   plane crash

5. People called Roberto _____.   golf balls

6. People all over the world named _____ after him.   ~~Puerto Rico~~

7. In 1972 there were three earthquakes in _____.   "The Great One"

8. Roberto died in a _____.   hospitals

94

Extension

GAMES

People play many different games. What are the most popular games in your home country?

Find out more about your favorite games. Share what you learn with the class. Follow these steps:

1. Choose a game that you want to learn more about.
2. Talk to your family and friends. Ask them about the game.
3. Find information about the game in books or on the Internet.
4. Make a poster about the game.
5. Write the rules of the game on a sheet of paper. Tape the rules to your poster.
6. Write the names of important players on the poster. Add pictures if you can.
7. Give an oral report about your game to the class. Show your poster.

Connect to Writing

GRAMMAR

Information Questions

Information questions begin with a question word. Many information questions in the simple past use *did* before the subject. For the main verb in the question, use the base form. Do not use -*ed* or an irregular past-tense ending.

Information Questions			Answers
question word	subject	main verb	
What did the ball		**do?**	It **bounced** up and down.
Where did the Aztecs		**live?**	They **lived** in what is now Mexico.
When did explorers		**go** to the Americas?	They **went** in the early 1500s.
Who did explorers		**meet** there?	They **met** Aztecs and Mayas.
How did the Olmecs		**make** rubber?	They **made** it from sap.
Why did ballplayers		**wear** pads?	They **wore** pads for protection.

Practice

Read the statements below. In your notebook, write the correct question word in the blank to complete each question. Use the underlined words to help you.

1. The Aztecs and Mayas played <u>games with a rubber ball</u>.
   *What* did the Aztecs and Mayas play?

2. Explorers went to the Americas <u>to look for gold</u>.
   _____ did explorers go to the Americas?

3. <u>In 1989</u>, scientists found three ancient rubber balls.
   _____ did scientists find three ancient rubber balls?

4. The Mayas and Aztecs played ball <u>on a court</u>.
   _____ did the Mayas and Aztecs play ball?

5. Scientists know <u>from their artifacts</u> that the Olmecs had rubber.
   _____ do scientists know the Olmecs had rubber?

6. The Olmecs came before <u>the Aztecs and the Mayas</u>.
   _____ did the Olmecs come before?

SKILLS FOR WRITING

Writing a Biographical Narrative

A biographical narrative tells the true story of a real person's life. It usually includes a problem that the person had to solve. Writers usually tell events in a biographical narrative in chronological order—in the order that they happened.

Read the example below about Olympic athlete Wilma Rudolph. Then answer the questions.

Alejandro Landin

Wilma Rudolph: Olympic Champion

Wilma Rudolph was born in Tennessee in 1940. As a child, she became sick with polio. Her doctor said she would never walk again. But Wilma was strong and worked hard. By age 11, she could walk without help. Wilma became a star runner and basketball player in high school. In 1956, she won a bronze medal in the women's 400-meter relay in the Olympic Games in Melbourne. Four years later, in the Olympic Games in Rome, Wilma won gold medals in the 100-meter and 200-meter dash, and the women's 400-meter relay. She was the first American woman to win three gold medals! Wilma wrote her autobiography, Wilma, in 1977. She was elected to the U.S. Olympic Hall of Fame in 1983.

1. How old was Wilma when she ran in the Melbourne Olympics?
2. How old was she when she won three gold medals in the Rome Olympics?
3. What problem did Wilma have? How did she solve it?

WRITING PRACTICE

Biographical Narrative

You will write a biographical narrative of someone you think is a hero.

1. **Read** Reread the biographical narrative on page 97. Then think of a hero to write about. It can be someone you know or someone you have read about.

Writing Strategy: Timeline

Before you write, make a timeline to organize the important events in chronological order. Read the timeline Alejandro used for his biographical narrative about Wilma Rudolph.

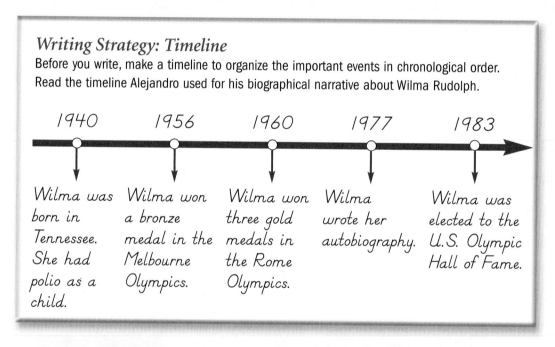

1940	1956	1960	1977	1983
Wilma was born in Tennessee. She had polio as a child.	Wilma won a bronze medal in the Melbourne Olympics.	Wilma won three gold medals in the Rome Olympics.	Wilma wrote her autobiography.	Wilma was elected to the U.S. Olympic Hall of Fame.

2. **Make a timeline** Think about the person you will write about. Make a timeline of important events. Include a problem the person had.

3. **Write** Use your timeline to write a biographical narrative. Tell the important events in chronological order. Talk about a problem and how the person solved it.

Link the Readings

Make a chart like the one below to compare the readings in this unit. Look at each word in the column. Put an **X** under "The Bouncing Ball" if the word reminds you of that selection. Put an **X** under "Roberto Clemente" if the word reminds you of the biography. Put an **X** in both places if the word reminds you of both selections.

	"The Bouncing Ball"	"Roberto Clemente"
explorers	_____	_____
major league	_____	_____
statue	_____	_____
artifact	_____	_____
achievement	_____	_____
opportunity	_____	_____
ruins	_____	_____
home run	_____	_____

Check Your Knowledge

Language Development
1. How did asking questions help you to understand the reading?
2. What is a biography?
3. How do you form an information question in the simple past? Give an example.
4. What is a timeline? What does it help you to do?

Academic Content
1. Describe a ball game that the Mayas and Aztecs played.
2. What did the Spanish think of the rubber ball when they first saw it?
3. What can we learn from artifacts?
4. What modern games are like the Aztec and Maya ball game? Explain.

Family Ties

SELECTION 1 "The Clever Daughter-in-Law"

SELECTION 2 "Family Traits"

In "The Clever Daughter-in-Law," a father wants his three sons to marry. The story has a riddle, or puzzle, in it. One girl answers the riddle and surprises everyone.

Grandparents, parents, and children often have many things in common. Their eye color or hair color may be the same. "Family Traits" tells about how people in families are alike.

OBJECTIVES

LANGUAGE DEVELOPMENT

Reading:
- **Vocabulary building:**
  Visual cues, dictionary skills
- **Reading strategies:**
  Predict, reread
- **Text types:**
  Folktale, drama, science text

Writing:
- ***Wh-* question chart**
- **Personal letter**

Listening/Speaking:
- **Retell a folktale**
- **Dramatize**

Grammar:
- **Adverbs**

Viewing/Representing:
- **Charts, diagrams, illustrations**
- **Family tree**

ACADEMIC CONTENT

- **Science vocabulary**
- **Family traits**
- **Gregor Mendel**

Prepare to Read

"The Clever Daughter-in-Law" is a folktale from China.
China is a large country in Asia.

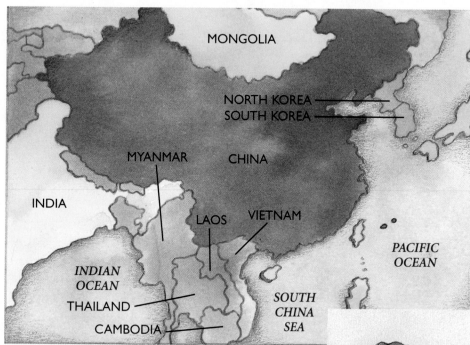

MONGOLIA

NORTH KOREA

SOUTH KOREA

MYANMAR   CHINA

INDIA

LAOS   VIETNAM

PACIFIC
OCEAN

INDIAN
OCEAN

THAILAND

CAMBODIA

SOUTH
CHINA
SEA

USE WHAT YOU KNOW

1 What do you know about China?

2 Look at the picture of the girl. What is she doing?

▲ Chinese farm girl from long ago

102

LEARN KEY WORDS

clever
daughter-in-law
father-in-law
lantern
missed

VOCABULARY

Look at the pictures and the captions. They will help you learn the words in the box. Write the meaning of each word. Then check your work in a dictionary.

▲ Chinese **lantern**

▲ A wife calls her husband's father **father-in-law**. She is his **daughter-in-law**. One daughter-in-law in this story is **clever,** or smart.

◀ The sisters **missed** their mother, so they asked their father-in-law if they could go to see her.

READING STRATEGY

Predict

To **predict** means to guess what will happen.

- Look for clues in the story and in the pictures.
- Think about what will happen next.
- At the end of the story, see if what you predicted was correct.

Folktale

"The Clever Daughter-in-Law" has a riddle, or puzzle, in it. This makes the folktale fun to tell. As you read, see if you can predict the ending of the story.

The Clever Daughter-in-Law

Adapted from *Celebrate the World: Twenty Tellable Folktales for Multicultural Festivals*, by Margaret Read MacDonald

Long, long ago in China, there was a rich old man. He lived in a big house. He had three sons. One day he said to his sons, "It is time for you to marry. I am getting old. I need a big family around me to help me in my old age."

Two of the sons found lovely wives. The two wives were sisters from a family in the next town. Soon the sisters came to live in the big house with their new husbands and their father-in-law. The old man was very happy. But he still needed to find a wife for his third son.

The two sisters liked the big new house, but they missed their mother terribly. Every month they wanted to visit her. "Kind Father-in-law," they said, "may we go home again for a few days?" The old man agreed, but he did not like them to go away so often.

CHECK YOUR UNDERSTANDING

Why does the rich old man want his sons to marry?

One day the old man had an idea. The two sisters came as usual and said, "Kind Father-in-law, may we go to visit our mother for a few days?"

"Of course," said the old man. "But please bring me two gifts when you return."

"Certainly," said the young wives. They wanted to please their father-in-law. "What gifts may we bring you?" they asked.

To the first wife the old man said, "You must bring me the wind wrapped in paper." And to the second wife he said, "You must bring me fire wrapped in paper." The two sisters were shocked. They left quickly. Then they walked along the road **silently** for some time.

"How can I find wind wrapped in paper?" the first sister asked.

"How can I find fire wrapped in paper?" asked the second sister. Neither sister had an answer. They sat down under a tree and began to cry loudly.

Soon a young farm girl saw them. She was walking with her **water buffalo**. "Why are you crying?" she asked. The sisters told her of the gifts they needed for their father-in-law. "Is that all?" the girl asked. "I can help you. Go to visit your mother and enjoy yourselves. I will have the gifts ready for you when you return."

---

silently, very quietly
water buffalo, large buffalo of Asia, often used as a farm animal

TRY TO PREDICT

What gifts do you think the farm girl will have ready for the sisters?

The two sisters returned the next day. The farm girl was waiting. "Here is the wind wrapped in paper," she said. In her hand was a paper fan. It made a gentle **breeze** when she waved it. Then she said, "And here is fire wrapped in paper." This time she held up a paper lantern with a bright candle inside.

"What a clever girl you are!" said the sisters. "Thank you so much!" They took the gifts and walked quickly back to the big house.

"Did you bring me the gifts?" asked the old man.

"Yes, good Father-in-law," said the two wives.

"Here is the wind wrapped in paper," said the first wife, and she showed him the fan.

"And here is fire wrapped in paper," said the second wife, and she showed him the lantern.

"How clever you are!" said the old man. "How did you think of these things?"

"Oh, we are not the clever ones," they said. "The young girl with the water buffalo was the clever one."

The old man invited the clever girl to meet his third son. They liked each other right away. Soon they married.

"How lucky I am," said the old father. "Now I have a happy house and a clever new daughter-in-law."

---

breeze, mild wind

MAKE CONNECTIONS

1. Does the clever farm girl remind you of anyone you know? Describe the person.

2. The farm girl solved the riddle. Do you know any riddles? Share them with a partner.

The Clever Daughter-in-Law

 A Play

Now read the same folktale as a play. There are six parts.

CHARACTERS

Narrator	**Young Wife 2**
Old Man	**Farm Girl**
Young Wife 1	**Chorus**

Narrator: Long, long ago in China, there was a rich old man with three sons. Two of the sons married sisters from the next town. The sisters came to live in the big house.

Old Man: I am very happy. But I still must find a wife for my third son.

Narrator: The wives missed their mother.

Young Wife 1: Kind Father-in-law, may we go to visit our mother for a few days?

Chorus: The old man did not like his daughters-in-law to go away so often. He had an idea.

Old Man: You may go, but please bring me two gifts when you return.

Young Wife 2: Certainly. What may we bring to you?

Old Man: First wife, you bring me the wind wrapped in paper. Second wife, you bring me fire wrapped in paper.

Chorus: The two sisters were shocked. They left quickly.

Young Wife 1 *(crying):* How can I find wind wrapped in paper?

Young Wife 2 *(crying):* How can I find fire wrapped in paper?

Narrator: A young farm girl saw them. She was walking with her water buffalo.

Farm Girl: Why are you crying?

Chorus: The sisters told her their problem.

Farm Girl: Is that all? Go visit your mother. I will have the gifts ready when you return.

Narrator: The next day the two sisters returned. The farm girl was waiting.

Farm Girl *(holding out a fan):* Here is the wind wrapped in paper.

Young Wife 1: Oh, thank you. You are so clever!

Farm Girl *(holding up a lantern with a candle):* And here is fire wrapped in paper.

Young Wife 2: What a clever girl you are! Thank you so much!

Narrator: They took the gifts and walked quickly back to the big house.

Old Man: Did you bring me the gifts?

Chorus: They showed him the fan and the lantern.

Old Man: How clever you are! How did you think of these things?

Young Wife 1: Oh, we are not the clever ones. It was a farm girl.

Narrator: The old man invited the clever girl to meet his third son. They liked each other right away. Soon they married.

Old Man: How lucky I am! Now I have a happy house and a clever new daughter-in-law.

Review and Practice

RETELL AND REVIEW

1. Look back at the pictures in "The Clever Daughter-in-Law" on pages 104–106. Cover the words on each page. Retell the story to a partner, using only the pictures.

2. What did the farm girl do that was clever? Explain.

3. What gifts did you predict the farm girl would have ready for the sisters?

COMPREHENSION

Write the sentences below in your notebook. Write *Yes* if the statement is true. Write *No* if it is not true. Then rewrite the statement correctly. Reread pages 104–106 to check your answers.

1. The rich old man lived in ancient Greece. *No. The rich old man lived in ancient China.*

2. Two of his sons married two sisters.

3. The young wives never left the big house.

4. The sisters wanted to visit their brother.

5. The old man asked for three gifts.

6. The old man wanted the wind wrapped in fire.

7. A farm girl was walking with her horse.

8. The paper lantern had a candle in it.

9. The farm girl was very clever.

10. The farm girl married the first son.

Extension

CHINESE LANTERN FESTIVAL

A. Read about a special Chinese festival.

The Chinese have a special lantern festival called *Yuanxiao Jie*. The Lantern Festival takes place on the fifteenth day of the first month of the Chinese New Year. People hang colorful lanterns in houses and buildings to celebrate the full moon and new year. Other people make lanterns and carry them on streets and in parks. Everyone comes out at night to see the colorful lanterns. People also watch dragon dances, play games, and light firecrackers. The Lantern Festival is a fun time for young and old.

▲ Paper lanterns in a temple during the Lantern Festival

People eat a special food called *yuanxiao*—named for the Lantern Festival. Yuanxiao is a kind of round dumpling made of sticky rice. One kind of yuanxiao is sweet and has nuts or fruit inside. Another kind is salty and has meat or vegetables inside.

B. Work in small groups. Take turns. Talk about a special festival in your home country. Answer these questions about the festival.

1. Where do people celebrate the festival?
2. When do they celebrate it?
3. What special activities do people do?
4. What special food do they eat?
5. Are there special customs for the festival?

Prepare to Read

"Family Traits" is nonfiction. It explains why children look so much like their parents. It is the kind of text you find in a science book.

▲ Do you think these young men are brothers? Why or why not?

▲ Do you think these baby ducks have the same parents? Why or why not?

▲ Why do you think this flower is the color it is?

USE WHAT YOU KNOW

What do you think makes people or animals in the same family look alike?

LEARN KEY WORDS

experiments
generations
inherit
members
traits

VOCABULARY

Look at the pictures and the captions. They will help you learn the words in the box. Write the meaning of each word. Then check your work in a dictionary.

▲ Family **members** make up a family. There are three **generations** in this family. The grandparents are one generation. Their son and his wife are a second generation. Their daughters are a third generation.

▲ These twins look alike. They have the same **traits**. Children **inherit,** or get, traits from their parents.

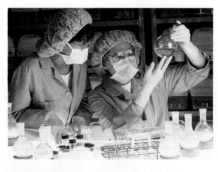

◄ Scientists test their ideas by doing **experiments**. Experiments help scientists learn about the world.

READING STRATEGY

Reread

To **reread** means to read again. Each time you read the text, you figure out a little more.

- Stop if you don't understand what you are reading.
- Reread sentences and paragraphs slowly.
- Reread key words and headings.

"Family Traits" tells why people in a family look alike. Read the text slowly. Reread any parts that you don't understand.

FAMILY TRAITS

What Are Family Traits?

Family traits are ways in which family members are alike. You may have the same color hair as your mother. You may have the same color eyes as your father. Eye color and hair color are family traits. Another family trait is how tall you are. Traits like these are passed on through families. You inherit, or get, these traits from your parents and your grandparents. You will pass on these traits to your own children.

> **MAKE CONNECTIONS**
>
> What family traits did you inherit from your parents or grandparents? Explain.

◀ These twins inherited the same traits from their parents and their grandparents. That is why they look alike.

▲ How can green birds have a blue chick?
Read the rest of this text to find out.

Do Children Always Look Like Their Parents?

Sometimes children do not look like their parents. For example, parents with brown eyes can have a child with blue eyes. This happens with other animals and even plants, too.

Look at the chart above. It shows that two green birds had four chicks. Three of the chicks are green, and one chick is blue. How can a chick inherit blue feathers when its parents' feathers are green? Many people wondered about this question. One of these people was a man named Gregor Mendel.

DISCUSS

Two orange cats can have a gray kitten. How is this idea like the idea of green birds having a blue chick?

Who Was Gregor Mendel?

Gregor Mendel (1822–1884) was a scientist and a monk who worked with plants. Mendel wanted to learn more about inherited traits. How can a trait that you cannot see in parents be passed on to their young? He did many experiments with pea plants. Mendel worked hard to find out the answer.

What Did Mendel Learn about Traits?

Mendel grew many generations of pea plants. Most of the pea-plant flowers were red, but some were white. This made him think that the trait for red flowers was stronger than the trait for white flowers. His experiments showed that this was true. In pea-plant flowers, redness is a strong, or dominant, trait. Whiteness is a weak, or recessive, trait.

Mendel believed that each trait was **determined** by a pair of **factors**. Each parent passes on one factor for every trait to its young. The way the factors combine determines what its young will look like. Today we call these factors genes.

---

determined, decided
factors, things that produce a result

▲ Gregor Mendel in his garden

114

When Do Recessive Traits Appear?

Look at the chart of Mendel's flowers. In the top row are a red and a white flower. This is the first generation. The red flower has two dominant genes (RR). The white flower has two recessive genes (rr). In the next row is the second generation. All the flowers are red because they have one dominant gene and one recessive gene (Rr). The dominant gene determines the color of the flower in these cases.

In the third generation one white flower appears. That flower is white because it has two recessive genes (rr). Mendel learned that the recessive color white appears only when there is no dominant gene (R) present in the pair.

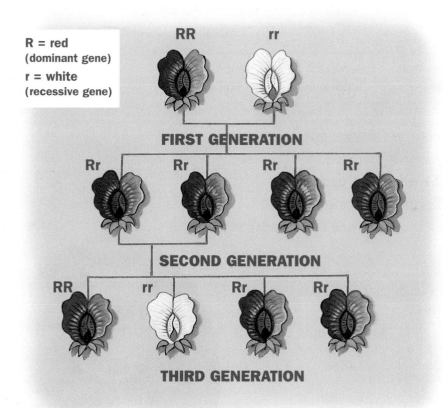

R = red
(dominant gene)

r = white
(recessive gene)

RR   rr

FIRST GENERATION

Rr   Rr   Rr   Rr

SECOND GENERATION

RR   rr   Rr   Rr

THIRD GENERATION

◀ This chart shows how pea-plant flowers pass on traits for the colors red and white.

CHECK YOUR UNDERSTANDING

Why are there so many more red pea-plant flowers than white?

115

Review and Practice

RETELL AND REVIEW

1. Tell a partner what you know about family traits. Use the headings and the pictures on pages 112–115 to help you.

2. Which parts of "Family Traits" did you reread? How did rereading help you understand the text?

COMPREHENSION

Write the sentences below in your notebook. Use the words in the box to complete the sentences.

recessive	family trait	dominant	genes
generation	inherit	experiments	members

1. Children are in a different *generation* than their parents.

2. One _____ is the color of your eyes.

3. We _____ family traits from our parents.

4. Redness is a _____ trait in pea-plant flowers.

5. _____ traits do not show up if one of the genes in a pair is dominant.

6. Brothers and sisters are _____ of the same family.

7. The pea-plant flower is white because it has two recessive _____ (rr).

8. Gregor Mendel did _____ to learn about dominant and recessive traits.

▲ Gregor Mendel

Extension

FAMILY TREE

A family tree is a chart of family information. It usually has names and birth dates. The top row on the chart shows grandparents. The next row shows parents. The bottom row shows children.

1. Copy the chart below on a large sheet of paper. It is an outline for a family tree.

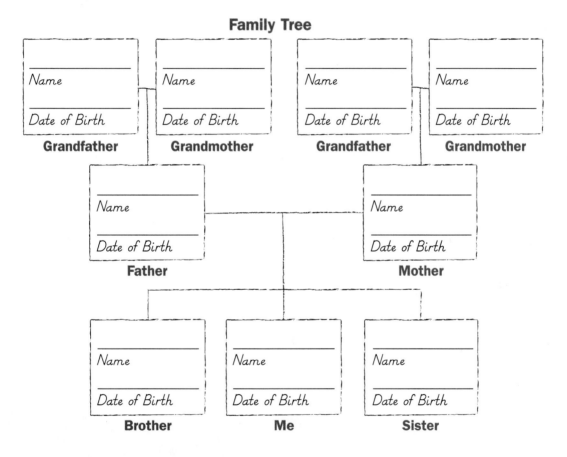

Family Tree

2. Write the names and birth dates of family members in the boxes. Ask people in your family questions to learn more about them. Write information about each family member. Leave places blank if you do not know the information.

3. Add a photo of your family or draw a picture.

4. Share your family tree with others. Compare information about your families.

5. Display your family tree.

Connect to Writing

GRAMMAR

Adverbs

Adverbs usually describe the action of verbs. They tell *how* an action happens. Many adverbs end in *–ly*.

> The sisters walked **quietly**.
>
> The scientist worked **carefully**.

Some adverbs have irregular forms. They do not end in *-ly*.

> The boys ran **fast**.
>
> John got 100 on the math test. He did **well**.
>
> Jane and I studied **hard**. We did **well** on the test.

Practice

Write these sentences in your notebook. Underline the adverbs.

1. The two sisters missed their mother terribly.
2. The old man spoke carefully.
3. The sisters cried loudly.
4. A young farm girl answered the questions cleverly.
5. The sisters ran home happily.
6. Gregor Mendel thought seriously about the problem.
7. He carefully grew many generations of pea plants.
8. Mendel worked hard and did his experiments well.

SKILLS FOR WRITING

Writing a Personal Letter

You write personal letters to your family members or close friends.

Read Sam's letter to his grandmother. Then discuss the questions.

November 5, 2004

Dear Grandma,

How are you doing? I am doing well.

My class learned about family history. We will make family trees. Can you tell me about our family history? Here is what I need to know. Who is in your family? What are your brothers' and sisters' names? Where were your brothers and sisters born? Where do they live now? Also, what are your parents' names? Where were they born? When did our family come to America? Why did we come here?

Please send me some family photos. I would really like one of you as a little girl. I will put the photos on my family tree. Will I see you soon? I hope so. I will show you my family tree.

Love,

Sam

1. What information does the writer need?
2. What are some questions the writer asks?
3. Find a sentence with an adverb in it. What verb does it describe?

WRITING PRACTICE

Personal Letter

You will write a personal letter to a family member to learn about your family history.

1. Read Reread the letter on page 119. Notice how the writer asks questions.

Writing Strategy: **Wh- Question Chart**

A *wh-* question chart can help you list the questions you need to ask. Look at the chart Sam used before writing his letter.

Who:	Who is in your family?
What:	What are your brothers' and sisters' names? What are your parents' names?
Where:	Where were your brothers and sisters born? Where do they live now?
When:	When did our family come to America?
Why:	Why did our family come to America?

---

2. Make a chart Make a *wh-* question chart listing the questions you will ask a family member. What can he or she tell you about your family?

3. Write Write a personal letter like Sam's. Include the questions from your chart.

Link the Readings

Make a chart like the one below to compare the readings in this unit. Look at each word in the column. Put an **X** under "The Clever Daughter-in-Law" if the word reminds you of the folktale. Put an **X** under "Family Traits" if the word reminds you of that selection. Put an **X** in both places if the word reminds you of both selections.

	"The Clever Daughter-in-Law"	"Family Traits"
fiction	_____	_____
nonfiction	_____	_____
traits	_____	_____
lantern	_____	_____
dominant	_____	_____
recessive	_____	_____
family	_____	_____

Check Your Knowledge

Language Development
1. Did any of the people in the folktale remind you of yourself or your own family members? Explain.
2. How is the farm girl in "The Clever Daughter-in-Law" like Ali in the folktale "Jewel in the Sand"? In what ways were they both clever?
3. What is an adverb? Use an adverb in a sentence.

Academic Content
1. Why do some twins look so much alike?
2. What are some inherited traits?
3. Who was Gregor Mendel? What did his experiments with pea plants show?

UNIT 5

THE POWER OF WORDS

SELECTION 1 "Early Writing"

SELECTION 2 "The Great Minu"

The selection "Early Writing" tells how the people of ancient Sumer created the first known form of writing.

Sometimes it is hard to understand another language. "The Great Minu" is a story about a man who hears a word from a different language and gets confused.

OBJECTIVES
LANGUAGE DEVELOPMENT

Reading:
- **Vocabulary building:**
  Visual cues, dictionary skills
- **Reading strategies:**
  Take notes, understand irony
- **Text types:**
  Social studies text, folktale, drama

Writing:
- **Subtopic web**
- **Report**

Listening/Speaking:
- **Retell a story**
- **Discuss**
- **Dramatize**

Grammar:
- **Pronouns**

Viewing/Representing:
- **Symbols, charts, maps, illustrations**

ACADEMIC CONTENT
- **Social studies vocabulary**
- **Ancient Sumer**
- **Cuneiform**

123

Prepare to Read

"Early Writing" is nonfiction. It tells about real things, people, and events. Writing began thousands of years ago in different places. One of these places was Sumer. Sumer was a country in what is now Iraq, in the Middle East.

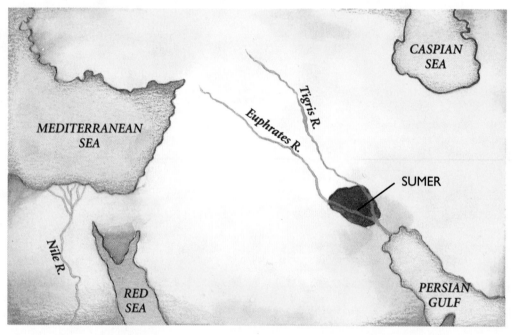

▲ The Tigris and Euphrates Rivers flowed through Sumer. The land was good for farming.

TRY TO PREDICT

Why do you think people began writing?

124

LEARN KEY WORDS

cuneiform
grain
reeds
symbols
wedges

VOCABULARY

Look at the pictures and the captions. They will help you learn the words in the box. Write the meaning of each word. Then check your work in a dictionary.

◀ People from ancient Sumer used a form of writing called **cuneiform** (kyoo-NEE-uh-form). Cuneiform was made of **symbols** shaped like **wedges**, or tiny triangles. Each symbol stood for a word.

▲ Some farmers in ancient Sumer grew **grain**. Grains are seeds that people eat, such as rice, wheat, and barley.

▲ **Reeds** are plants that grow in or near water.

READING STRATEGY

Take Notes

To **take notes** means to write down important ideas as you read. Taking notes can help you remember important facts from the text.

- Write only the most important words.
- You can shorten some words, such as *cune* for *cuneiform.*
- Reread your notes when you finish the text.

"Early Writing" tells how an ancient form of writing began. As you read, look for important ideas. Write them in your notebook. Look at your notes after you finish reading.

EARLY WRITING

Why Did People Begin Writing?

Over five thousand years ago, people living in Sumer created the first known form of writing. What made these people begin to write?

Many Sumerians were farmers. Some farmers grew grain, such as barley, for food. Other farmers raised sheep for milk and wool. As Sumer got bigger, its people needed a way to record, or write down, facts about their **products**. For example, farmers needed to know how much grain or how many sheep they had. When farmers **traded** barley or sheep for other products, they needed a way to remember how much grain and how many animals they had traded.

Writing was a way for Sumerians to record facts and remember them. Perhaps writing began when a sheep farmer drew a picture of a sheep. Then he added marks next to it to show how many he had traded.

▲ This Sumerian clay tablet tells how many sheep and goats people had.

CHECK YOUR UNDERSTANDING

What kind of information did farmers in Sumer need to record?

---

products, things people make or grow
traded, bought and sold

126

How Did the Sumerians Write?

The Sumerians did not have paper to write on as we do today. They wrote on clay tablets—flat pieces of clay. There was a lot of clay along the Tigris and Euphrates Rivers, where many Sumerians lived. Wet clay was soft and easy to write on. When the clay dried in the sun, it became hard and strong.

The Sumerians wrote on clay with reeds, plants that grew along the rivers. They pressed the end of a reed into the clay and made pictures and marks. The marks were shaped like wedges, or small triangles. We call these marks cuneiform. *Cuneiform* comes from two Latin words: *cuneus,* which means "wedge," and *forma,* which means "shape."

▲ Reeds grew along the Tigris and Euphrates Rivers.

▲ Sumerians wrote on clay with a reed. The reed made wedge-shaped marks in the clay.

CHECK YOUR UNDERSTANDING

1 Why did the Sumerians write on clay?

2 What does the word *cuneiform* mean?

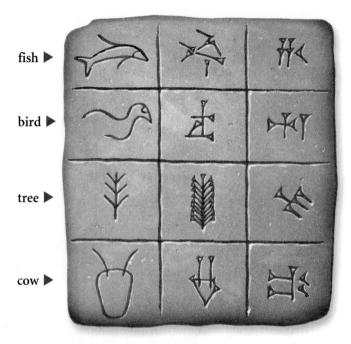

fish ▶
bird ▶
tree ▶
cow ▶

◀ This tablet shows how the pictures used in early Sumerian writing changed over time into wedge-shaped cuneiform.

How Did Sumerian Writing Change over Time?

The earliest Sumerian writing was made up of little pictures. The pictures stood for things and for the sounds of words for those things. For example, the symbol 〰 could mean the idea of water and the sound of the word for water in the Sumerian language.

Over time, the pictures changed to cuneiform. Cuneiform was easier and faster for people to write. Look at the tablet above. It shows how the pictures for *fish, bird, tree,* and *cow* changed over time.

▲ Cuneiform writing on a wall in the Palace of Darius I, Persepolis, Iran

MAKE CONNECTIONS

What is the writing like in your home country? Explain.

How Did the Sumerians Write Numbers?

The Sumerians also used cuneiform to write numbers. One vertical, or up-and-down, wedge mark stood for the number 1, two vertical wedge marks stood for the number 2, and so on. One sideways wedge mark stood for the number 10.

Over time, trade in Sumer grew. The people needed to use larger numbers. People began to use the symbol ⟆ to stand for both 1 and 60. How did they do this? A ⟆ symbol on the left side of a number stood for 60. On the right side of a number, the same symbol stood for 1. For an example, see the number 201 in cuneiform below.

▲ This tablet tells how many workers were given certain jobs to do.

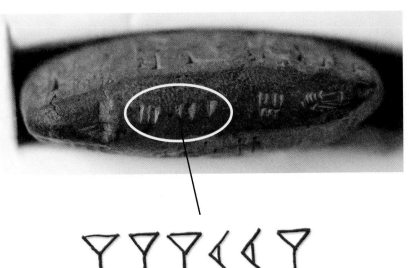

◀ The edge of the tablet shows the total number of workers: 201.

60 + 60 + 60 + 10 + 10 + 1 = 201

CHECK YOUR UNDERSTANDING

How did Sumerians change the way they wrote over time?

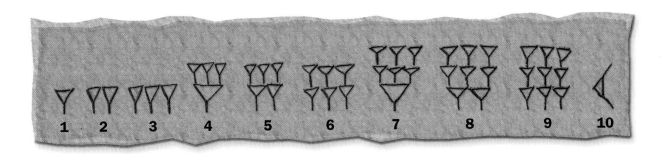

| 1 | 2 | 3 | 4 | 5 | 6 | 7 | 8 | 9 | 10 |

Review and Practice

1. Tell a partner what you learned about early Sumerian writing and cuneiform. Use the headings and the pictures on pages 126–129 to help you.

2. What important words and ideas did you write down as you read the text? Did you shorten words as you took notes?

COMPREHENSION

Write the sentences below in your notebook. Write *Yes* if the statement is true. Write *No* if it is not true. Then rewrite the statement correctly. Reread pages 126–129 to check your answers.

1. Sumerians used tree branches to write on clay. *No. Sumerians used reeds to write on clay.*

2. Sumerians first used writing to record facts about products they traded.

3. Farmers in Sumer grew barley, a kind of reed.

4. The earliest symbols used in Sumerian writing were little pictures.

5. In Sumer, people wrote on paper.

6. There were no rivers in Sumer.

7. Cuneiform symbols were shaped like wedges.

8. The same wedge-shaped symbol could stand for both the numbers 1 and 60.

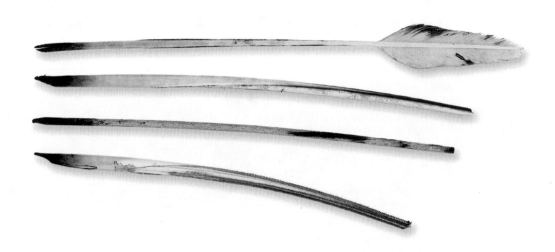

Extension

OTHER EARLY WRITING

The Sumerians created one form of writing. Other ancient peoples wrote in other ways. They used different materials to write with and to write on. They used different symbols. Look at the examples below.

▲ Ancient Egyptian writing

▲ Ancient Chinese writing

◀ Ancient Arabic writing

A. Talk about the early forms of writing in small groups.

1. Describe the symbols. What shapes are they?
2. What do you think the people wrote with?
3. What material did they write on?

B. Find out more about early forms of writing.

1. Use the library or the Internet to find information.
2. Choose a place to read about, such as Sumer, Egypt, or China.
3. Take notes as you read.
4. Talk about what you have learned with a partner.

Prepare to Read

"The Great Minu" is a folktale from Ghana, a country in West Africa. Ghana has many regions, or parts. More than fifty languages were once spoken in these different regions. Today, children in Ghana learn English in school. It is now the main language in Ghana.

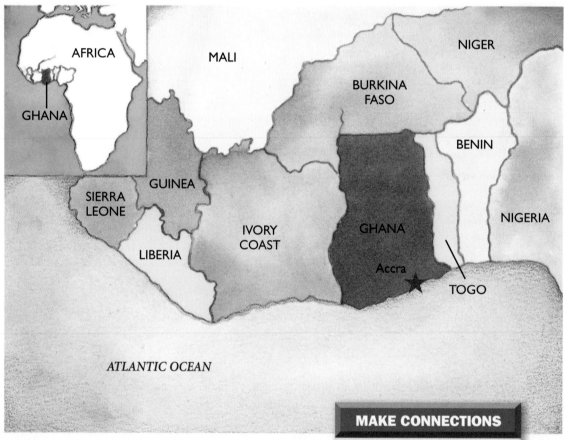

AFRICA

GHANA

MALI

NIGER

BURKINA FASO

BENIN

GUINEA

SIERRA LEONE

LIBERIA

IVORY COAST

GHANA

Accra

NIGERIA

TOGO

ATLANTIC OCEAN

▲ Ghana is a country in West Africa. Accra is the capital city of Ghana.

MAKE CONNECTIONS

1 What language or languages do you speak?

2 How do you say "hello" in your home language?

3 Does your home language use the same alphabet as English?

LEARN KEY WORDS

coffin
funeral
port
sailor
village

VOCABULARY

Look at the pictures and the captions. They will help you learn the words in the box. Write the meaning of each word. Then check your work in a dictionary.

▲ Many people walk behind the **coffin** during a **funeral**.

▲ A West African **village**

◄ The **sailor** works on a ship. The ship is in the **port**.

READING STRATEGY

Understand Irony

Sometimes you know something that a character in the story doesn't know. This is called **irony**. As you read, ask yourself:

- What does Akwasi think "Minu" means?
- What does the writer tell you "Minu" means?
- How does this irony make the story funny?

FOCUS ON LITERATURE ▸ **Folktale** •

This is a folktale about a man from a small village in Ghana. His name is Akwasi. Akwasi decides to travel to Accra, the capital city of Ghana. As you read, think about how the writer uses irony.

THE GREAT MINU

Adapted from *Folktales and Fairy Tales of Africa,* selected and retold by Lila Green

A long time ago, there was a young man named Akwasi (ah-KWAH-zee). Akwasi lived in a small village in Ghana. One day, Akwasi decided to travel to Accra, the capital city. It was a long way from his village. He had never been to Accra before. He did not know that the people of Accra spoke a different language.

Akwasi walked for many days. Finally, he arrived at the city of Accra. Just outside the city were hundreds of cows.

"Tell me, who owns all these cows?" he asked a young boy who was standing near the cows.

"Minu," the boy said, which in the language of Accra means, "I don't understand."

"Minu?" Akwasi said. "Minu must be a very rich man!"

CHECK YOUR UNDERSTANDING

Why is Akwasi confused?

Then Akwasi entered the city. He saw many big shops. The shops were full of beautiful things—rugs, gold jewelry, bells, lamps, and mirrors. In his small village, there were no shops like these.

Akwasi asked a woman, "Tell me, who owns all these beautiful shops?"

But the woman did not understand. "Minu," she said.

"Mr. Minu?" Akwasi said. "He owns all these shops, too? He really must be very, very rich!"

Next, Akwasi walked by some very large and fine houses.

"These houses are **magnificent**," he said. "They are not like the small **huts** in my village!"

Akwasi saw a young girl sweeping the steps of a big house.

"Tell me, who owns these houses?" he asked.

But the young girl did not understand. "Minu," she said.

"Minu," Akwasi repeated. "Of course, the great Mr. Minu!"

Then Akwasi arrived at the port. There were many ships. Akwasi could see that there were many boxes and bags of grain on the ships.

"Tell me, who owns all these ships?" Akwasi asked a sailor.

But the sailor did not understand. "Minu," he said.

"Is that so?" Akwasi said. "Mr. Minu owns these ships, too? Mr. Minu must be the richest man in the whole world!"

magnificent, grand, beautiful
huts, small houses with only one or two rooms

MAKE CONNECTIONS

Do you think Akwasi wants to be Mr. Minu? Why or why not?

After Akwasi had walked around Accra for a long, long time, he decided to go home. He wanted to be back in his own village. He began walking toward the edge of the city. Suddenly, he saw a long line of people. They were walking behind a coffin. Many of the people were crying.

"A funeral," Akwasi said to himself. "An important person must have died."

Akwasi stopped a woman who was in the long line of people. "Tell me," he said. "Who is the person who died?" But the woman did not understand.

"Minu," she said sadly.

"Oh, no!" Akwasi said. "The great Mr. Minu is dead! Can it be true? How sad! He owned hundreds of cows. He owned many beautiful shops. He owned magnificent houses. He owned many large ships. And now look at him! He is in a coffin. He has left all those fine things behind. He has died, just like any other person."

At that moment, Akwasi felt that it was not so bad to be just plain Akwasi, and not the great Mr. Minu. The more he thought about it, the more Akwasi understood that he had much to be thankful for. Akwasi felt that it was very good to be alive, even if he didn't own a lot of things. And so Akwasi walked back to his village, a happy man.

CHECK YOUR UNDERSTANDING

Why was Akwasi happy to be himself and not Mr. Minu at the end of the story?

The Great Minu ◆ A Play

Now read the same folktale as a play. There are eight parts.

CHARACTERS

Narrator	**Young Girl**
Akwasi	**Sailor**
Young Boy	**Second Woman**
First Woman	**Chorus**

Narrator: A long time ago, a young man named Akwasi lived in Ghana.

Chorus: His home was in a village.

Narrator: One day, Akwasi decided to travel to Accra, the capital city. The people there did not speak his language, but Akwasi did not know this.

Chorus: He traveled for many days.

Narrator: Finally, he arrived at the city. Just outside the city were hundreds of cows.

Akwasi *(to boy):* Who owns these cows?

Young Boy: Minu.

Akwasi: Minu? Minu must be a very rich man!

Narrator: Then Akwasi entered the city.

Chorus: He saw many big shops full of beautiful things.

Akwasi *(to woman):* Look at all these beautiful shops! Who owns all these shops?

First Woman: Minu.

Akwasi: Mr. Minu, again? Does he own these shops, too? He really must be very, very rich!

Narrator: Next, Akwasi passed some large and fine houses.

Chorus: He had never seen anything like them in his own village.

Narrator: He saw a young girl sweeping some steps.

Akwasi *(to girl):* These houses are magnificent. Who owns these houses?

Young Girl: Minu.

Akwasi: Minu. Of course, it is the great Mr. Minu!

Narrator: Then Akwasi arrived at the port.

Chorus: He saw many ships full of grain.

Akwasi *(to sailor):* Who owns all these ships?

Sailor: Minu.

Akwasi: Can it be true? Mr. Minu must be the richest man in the world!

Narrator: Finally, Akwasi decided to go home to his village. As he was leaving Accra, he passed a long line of people.

Chorus: They were walking behind a coffin.

Akwasi *(to woman):* This must be a funeral. What important person died?

Second Woman: Minu.

Akwasi: Oh, no! Is the great Mr. Minu dead?

Narrator: Akwasi thought about all Mr. Minu had owned.

Akwasi: Now look! He is dead, just like any other person.

Chorus: Akwasi went home to his village.

Akwasi: I am happy to be who I am. I have many things to be thankful for. It is good to be alive.

Review and Practice

RETELL AND REVIEW

1. Look back at the pictures in "The Great Minu" on pages 134–136. Cover the words on each page. Retell the events of the story to a partner, using only the pictures.
2. How does the writer use irony in the story?
3. What do you think is the lesson of this folktale?

COMPREHENSION

Complete the sentences. Choose the correct word from the column on the right. Write the completed sentences in your notebook.

1. Accra is the *capital* of Ghana.
2. The people of Accra did not speak Akwasi's _____.
3. Just outside the city, Akwasi saw hundreds of _____.
4. The shops were full of beautiful _____.
5. Akwasi talked to a young girl near one of the _____.
6. There were many bags of _____ on the ships.
7. People in the funeral walked behind a _____.
8. Akwasi traveled back home to his _____.

things
village
grain
language
coffin
~~capital~~
cows
houses

138

Extension

KENTE CLOTH

Artists in Ghana make kente cloths for people to wear. These cloths have many different designs. Each design means something different. Look at the examples below.

"Babadua"
strength

"Mother Hen"
good mothers

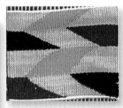
"Potsherd"
knowledge

"Rising Sun"
progress and energy

A. Talk about the kente cloths in small groups.

  1. What colors does each one include?

  2. What does each design mean?

  3. How are they the same? How are they different?

  4. Which is your favorite kente cloth? Explain why you like it.

B. Create your own kente cloth design.

  1. Choose three of four colors for your cloth. Create a pattern with the colors.

  2. Choose a meaning for your design.

  3. Draw your design on paper. The basic design should be 10 centimeters (4 in.) wide. Repeat the design to make the cloth wider.

  4. Share your kente cloth design with the class.

Connect to Writing

GRAMMAR

Pronouns

Pronouns are words that take the place of nouns. A **subject pronoun** replaces a noun that is the subject of a sentence.

subject   subject pronoun

Akwasi left his village. **He** left his village.

An **object pronoun** replaces a noun that is the object of a sentence.

object   object pronoun

People did not understand **Akwasi**. People did not understand **him**.

Subject Pronouns	Object Pronouns
I	me
you	you
he, she, it	him, her, it
we	us
you	you
they	them

Practice

Copy these sentences in your notebook. Replace the <u>underlined noun</u> in the first sentence with a pronoun in the second sentence.

1. Akwasi traveled to <u>Accra</u>. _____*It*_____ is the capital city of Ghana.

2. Akwasi asked people <u>questions</u>. The people of Accra could not understand _____.

3. Akwasi saw a <u>girl</u> sweeping the steps. Akwasi asked _____ a question.

4. <u>Akwasi</u> decided to leave Accra. _____ thought it was time to go home.

5. <u>You and I</u> learned a lesson from Akwasi. _____ can explain it to the teacher.

SKILLS FOR WRITING

Writing Notes for a Report

A report gives information about a topic. To write a report, first choose a topic. Then find information about that topic. Suppose your topic is "Ancient Egyptian Writing." You can find information about ancient Egypt in books and on the Internet.

As you find information, you need to organize it, or put it in order. One way to organize information is to write notes. Write notes for each book or website you use.

- Write down important facts and ideas.

- Use your own words. Do not copy information from a source.

- Write the address of the website. For a book, write the title, author, publisher, place and date of publication, and page number.

Read notes that one student wrote. Then answer the questions.

Ancient Egyptian Writing
- *earliest form called hieroglyphs*
- *Egyptians began writing hiero around 3000 B.C.E.*
- *Most were pictures that stood for people, animals, & things*
- *Hiero were painted, carved, or written with brush and ink*
Source: Ancient Egypt, by George Hart, Dorling Kindersley, New York, 1990, p. 34

---

1. What is the topic of this report?

2. What source (book or website) did the writer use for the notes?

3. Where did the student write the source?

WRITING PRACTICE

Report

You will write a report about an early form of writing.

1. **Read** Reread the student's notes on page 141. Think of a topic on early writing that you want to write about.

Writing Strategy: Subtopic Web

Think about your topic. What subtopics, or smaller topics, do you want to write about? Use a subtopic web to organize your ideas. Write your topic in the middle of a sheet of paper. Then think of some ideas to write about your topic. Look at this student's subtopic web.

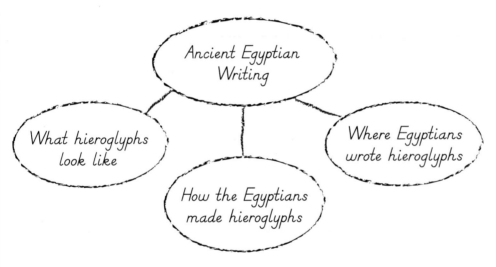

Look for information about your subtopics in the library and on the Internet. Which ideas can you find the most information about? Choose these subtopics to write about.

2. **Make a subtopic web** Make a subtopic web for your topic in your notebook. Choose three subtopics. Then find information about them. Remember to write notes and be sure to include source information.

3. **Write** Use your notes to write your report.

Link the Readings

Make a chart like the one below to compare the readings in this unit. Look at each word in the column. Put an **X** under "Early Writing" if the word reminds you of that text. Put an **X** under "The Great Minu" if the word reminds you of the folktale. Put an **X** in both places if the word reminds you of both selections.

	"Early Writing"	"The Great Minu"
grain	_____	_____
reeds	_____	_____
village	_____	_____
coffin	_____	_____
wedges	_____	_____
symbols	_____	_____
funeral	_____	_____

Check Your Knowledge

Language Development

1. Look at your notes from "Early Writing." Use your notes to tell a friend what you learned.
2. What is a pronoun? Say a sentence with a subject pronoun. Say a sentence with an object pronoun.
3. Describe the irony in the folktale "The Great Minu."

Academic Content

1. What modern country is located where ancient Sumer once was?
2. Why did the people of Sumer need writing?
3. How did the Sumerians write numbers?

EXPLORING THE SENSES

SELECTION 1 "The Blind Men and the Elephant"

SELECTION 2 "Animal Senses"

Sometimes we learn the truth about something by thinking about it in different ways. The fable "The Blind Men and the Elephant" is a story that teaches a lesson about "seeing" and understanding.

Animals use their senses to survive, or stay alive. Read "Animal Senses" to learn about some interesting ways animals use their hearing, smell, sight, and touch.

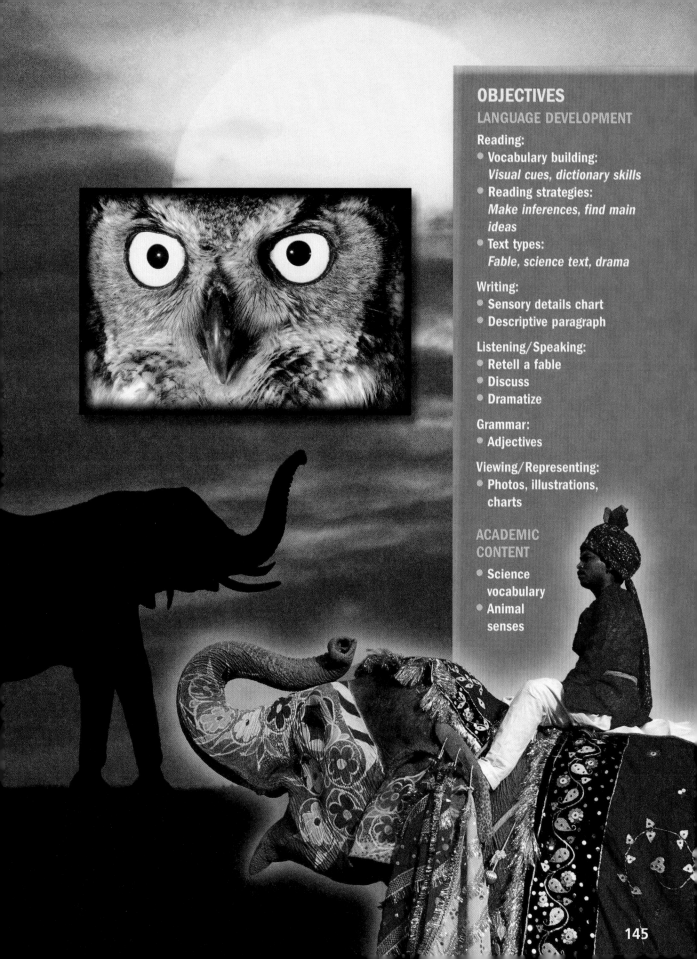

OBJECTIVES

LANGUAGE DEVELOPMENT

Reading:
- **Vocabulary building:**
  Visual cues, dictionary skills
- **Reading strategies:**
  Make inferences, find main ideas
- **Text types:**
  Fable, science text, drama

Writing:
- **Sensory details chart**
- **Descriptive paragraph**

Listening/Speaking:
- **Retell a fable**
- **Discuss**
- **Dramatize**

Grammar:
- **Adjectives**

Viewing/Representing:
- **Photos, illustrations, charts**

ACADEMIC CONTENT

- **Science vocabulary**
- **Animal senses**

Prepare to Read

"The Blind Men and the Elephant" is a fable. A fable is a story that teaches a moral, or a lesson about life. This fable is from India.

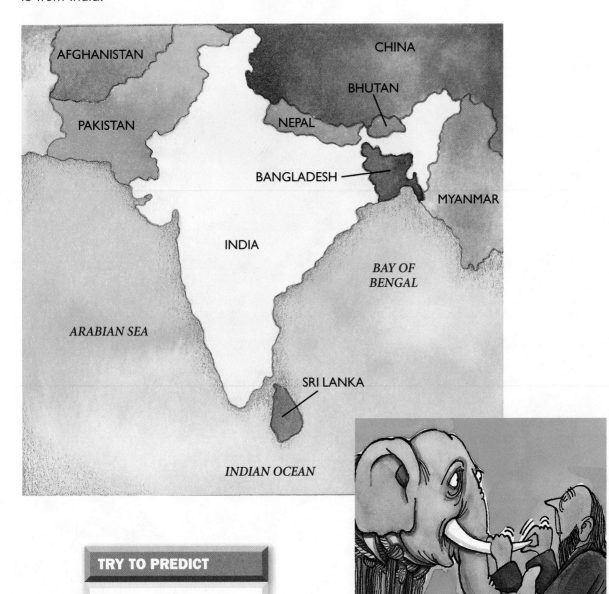

TRY TO PREDICT

Why do you think the man is touching the elephant? Explain.

146

LEARN KEY WORDS

argue
elephant
gentle
trunk
tusks

VOCABULARY

Look at the pictures and the captions. They will help you learn the words in the box. Write the meaning of each word. Then check your work in a dictionary.

▲ An **elephant** is a large animal. It has two long front teeth called **tusks** and a long nose called a **trunk**. The elephant in the story is a **gentle** animal. It does not hurt people.

▲ When people have different ideas, they sometimes **argue** about which idea is right.

READING STRATEGY

Make Inferences

Sometimes writers do not tell you what a story means. They give clues about the story's meaning. These clues can be things that the characters do and say. The reader uses the clues to **make inferences** about, or guess, the story's meaning.

- Look for clues in the story.
- Think about what the characters do and say.
- Use these clues to guess the meaning of the story.

147

Fable

"The Blind Men and the Elephant" is a fable from India. Like most fables, it has a moral, or a lesson about life. As you read, make inferences and guess the moral of the story.

The Blind Men and the Elephant

Once upon a time, six blind men were walking down a road in India. They met an old man leading an elephant. They stopped to speak to the old man. One of the blind men said, "Sir, what kind of animal do you have? It is making a **strange** noise."

The old man said, "It is an elephant."

"An elephant?" said one of the blind men. "I don't know what an elephant is."

"May we touch it?" asked the second blind man. "We want to know what an elephant is like."

"Of course," said the old man. "This elephant is gentle. It will not hurt you."

One by one, the blind men began to touch the elephant. The first blind man touched one of the elephant's tusks. It was long and smooth. The tip was pointed and sharp. He said, "An elephant is like a spear."

---

strange, not usual

MAKE CONNECTIONS

Have you ever seen an elephant? Where?

Then the second blind man touched the elephant's trunk. It was long and very strong. It moved up and down and from side to side. He cried, "Brothers, an elephant is not like a spear. It is like a snake!"

Next, the third blind man touched one of the elephant's legs. It felt thick and rough. It was very tall. "No, you are wrong, my brothers. An elephant is not like a spear. It is not like a snake, either. It is like a large tree."

After that, the fourth blind man touched the elephant's side. Then he said, "Are you crazy? An elephant is not like a spear. And it is not like a snake. It is not like a tree, either. It is hard and wide and flat. I cannot find the end of it. An elephant is like a great wall."

At that moment, the elephant lowered its head. The fifth blind man reached out and touched one of the elephant's ears. It felt big and soft and flat. It flapped and made a **breeze**. He said, "No, my brothers. An elephant is not like a spear or a snake or a tree or a wall. It is like a huge fan."

---

breeze, gentle wind

MAKE CONNECTIONS

Have you ever touched something at night that you couldn't see? Explain.

Finally, the sixth blind man touched the elephant's tail. It was long and thin. It had hair on the end. He said, "You are all wrong. An elephant is not like a spear or a snake or a tree or a wall, or even a fan. An elephant is like a rope."

Now, the blind men started to argue. Each one thought that his idea about an elephant was correct.

"Wait," said the old man with the elephant. "You are all right. But you are also all wrong."

The six men were confused. "How can we be right—and wrong?" they asked.

The old man replied, "Each of you touched only a part of the elephant. An elephant is more than a spear. It is more than a snake. It is more than a tree. It is more than a wall. It is more than a fan. It is more than a rope. **Imagine** an animal that is all of those things put together. Can you imagine something huge and strange? *That* is an elephant."

---

imagine, see in your mind, picture

DISCUSS

Why did the men argue about what an elephant is?

The Blind Men and the Elephant
 A Play

Now read the fable as a play. There are nine parts.

CHARACTERS

Narrator
First Blind Man
Elephant Keeper
Second Blind Man
Third Blind Man

Fourth Blind Man
Fifth Blind Man
Sixth Blind Man
Chorus

Narrator: Once upon a time, six blind men were walking down a road in India. They met an old man leading an elephant.

First Blind Man: Sir, what kind of animal do you have? It is making a strange noise.

Elephant Keeper: It is an elephant.

First Blind Man: An elephant? I don't know what an elephant is.

Second Blind Man: May we touch it? We want to know what an elephant is like.

Elephant Keeper: Of course. This elephant is very gentle. It will not hurt you.

Narrator: The blind men began to touch the elephant.

Chorus: The first blind man touched a tusk.

First Blind Man: It is long and pointed! This animal is like a spear.

Chorus: The second blind man touched the trunk.

Second Blind Man: It is long, and it moves up and down and from side to side! Brothers, this elephant is like a snake!

Chorus: The third blind man touched one of the elephant's legs.

Third Blind Man: It is thick and rough. No, brothers, an elephant is like a large tree.

Chorus: The fourth blind man touched the elephant's side.

Fourth Blind Man: Are you crazy? This animal is hard and wide and flat. An elephant is like a great wall.

Chorus: Then, the elephant lowered its head. The fifth blind man touched one of the elephant's ears.

Fifth Blind Man: It is big and flat. It makes a breeze. An elephant is like a fan.

Chorus: The sixth blind man touched the elephant's tail.

Sixth Blind Man: It is long and thin. It has hair on it. An elephant is like a rope.

Narrator: The blind men started to argue. Each one thought his idea about the elephant was right.

Elephant Keeper: Wait! You are all right. But you are also all wrong. Each of you touched only a part of the elephant.

Chorus: An elephant is more than a spear. It is more than a snake. It is more than a tree. It is more than a wall. It is more than a fan. It is more than a rope.

Elephant Keeper: Can you imagine an animal that is all of those things put together? Can you imagine something huge and strange? *That* is an elephant.

Review and Practice

RETELL AND REVIEW

1. Look back at the pictures in "The Blind Men and the Elephant" on pages 148–150. Cover the words on each page. Retell the events of the story to a partner, using only the pictures.

2. What is the moral of this fable? Explain how clues from the story helped you understand the moral.

COMPREHENSION

Complete the sentences. Choose the correct word from the column on the right. Write the completed sentences in your notebook.

1. This fable takes place in the country of ___India___.   fan
2. The six blind men did not know about _____.   ~~India~~
3. The first blind man thought the tusk was like a _____.   wall
4. The second blind man thought the trunk was like a _____.   snake
5. The third blind man thought the leg was like a _____.   rope
6. The fourth blind man thought the side was like a _____.   spear
7. The fifth blind man thought the ear was like a _____.   elephants
8. The sixth blind man thought the tail was like a _____.   tree

Extension

SIMILES

A simile shows how two things are alike, or similar. In a simile, you use the word *like* to compare two things.

The elephant's tail was *like* a rope.
(The simile compares the elephant's tail to a rope.)

A. Look at your completed Comprehension sentences from page 152. Find the similes in sentences 3–8. Then write in your notebook the two things that each simile compares.

The first blind man thought the tusk was like a spear.
The simile compares an elephant's tusk to a spear.

B. Read the poem. Then complete the activity.

Rain Poem

The rain was like a little mouse,
quiet, small and gray.
It pattered all around the house
and then it went away.

It did not come, I understand,
indoors at all, until
it found an open window and
left tracks across the **sill**.

—Elizabeth Coatsworth

_____

sill, bottom of a window

1. Underline the simile in the poem.
2. What two things are being compared?
3. Name three words that show how the two things are alike.

Prepare to Read

"Animal Senses" is a nonfiction text. It tells about the ways animals see, hear, smell, and touch.

Elephants cannot see very well. But they have good senses of smell, touch, and hearing. ▶

In what ways do elephants "talk" to each other?

154

LEARN KEY WORDS

hive
predators
prey
survive
vision

VOCABULARY

Look at the pictures and the captions. They will help you learn the words in the box. Write the meaning of each word. Then check your work in a dictionary.

▲ Bees live in a **hive**.

▲ Owls see well. Their good **vision** helps them find food to **survive**, or stay alive.

◀ Owls eat mice. Owls are **predators**. Mice are their **prey**.

READING STRATEGY

Find Main Ideas

The **main ideas** are the most important ideas in a text. Each paragraph usually has one main idea. The main ideas help you remember the important parts of the text.

- Notice headings and titles. They are clues to main ideas.
- Remember that the first sentence of a paragraph often tells the main idea.
- Look for facts that support the main idea in each paragraph.

Science

"Animal Senses" is a nonfiction text. It explains how three kinds of animals use their senses. As you read, look for main ideas in each section.

Animal Senses

Why Are Senses Important?

Animals use their senses to survive in nature. Animals' abilities to see, hear, smell, taste, and touch help them find food. Animals also use their senses to avoid, or stay away from, their enemies.

Animals **adapt** to their specific environments, or surroundings. As a result, most animals have one or two senses that are more important than the others. These senses help animals survive.

▲ A baby elephant feels safe holding onto its mother's tail.

How Do Elephants Use Their Senses of Smell and Touch?

Elephants have small eyes, and they cannot see well. They use their senses of smell and touch to find food, water, and other animals. Elephants breathe and smell with their trunks. They use their trunks to smell the air

Elephants use their trunks to smell the air and the ground. ▼

---

adapt, change to fit a specific situation better

CHECK YOUR UNDERSTANDING

Why don't elephants use their sense of vision to find food and water?

and the ground. Sometimes they can smell other animals or water from miles away.

Elephants also touch each other with their trunks to **communicate**. Friendly elephants touch trunks as a greeting. Mother elephants touch new baby elephants with their trunks to welcome them. When a baby elephant is afraid, the mother strokes it with her trunk. Sometimes a baby elephant holds its mother's tail with its trunk. That makes the baby feel safe.

How Do Elephants Feel with Their Feet?

Scientists think that elephants' feet can feel **vibrations** in the ground. For example, when thunder makes the ground shake far away, elephants feel the direction of the thunder with their feet. Then the elephants know where to find rainwater.

How Do Elephants Use Their Sense of Hearing?

Elephants use their sense of hearing to avoid danger. Elephants can hear low sounds that human ears can't. They can also make special low sounds with their trunks to communicate with other elephants far away. For example, elephants make sounds to tell other elephants about dangerous animals, such as lions. Baby elephants make special sounds when they are afraid. When a mother elephant hears the sounds, she goes to help her baby.

---

communicate, give or share information
vibrations, shaking movements

CHECK YOUR UNDERSTANDING

Name two ways elephants communicate with each other.

▲ Elephants' big ears can hear sounds that people's ears cannot hear.

▲ Elephants make sounds with their trunks to communicate with other elephants.

What Is Special about an Owl's Eyes?

Owls have excellent vision. At night, they fly and look for prey—small animals to eat, such as mice, rabbits, frogs, and birds. When owls see an animal move, they fly down and catch it.

Owls are predators—they catch and eat other animals. Their large eyes are specially adapted for **hunting** at night. Most birds have eyes on the sides of their head. These birds see well on the sides, but they do not see well in front of themselves. Owls are different. They have eyes in the front of their head, which makes them good hunters. Their eyes are good at following and catching prey.

---

hunting, catching and killing animals for food

▲ "Eyes in front, likes to hunt." Predators, such as owls, have eyes in the front of their head. Their front-facing eyes help them find and catch prey.

◀ "Eyes on the side, likes to hide." Many animals, such as this sparrow, have eyes on the sides of their head. Sparrows can see left and right, so they can escape from predators.

▲ Owls catch and eat mice, frogs, rabbits, and birds.

MAKE CONNECTIONS

1 Can you think of another bird or animal that has eyes in front?

2 In English, the sound an owl makes is, "Whooo!" What sound does an owl make in your first language?

Why Do Honeybees Dance?

Honeybees live together in large groups in hives. Honeybees travel to different flowers to get food and **nectar**. They use the nectar to make honey inside the hive. Honeybees cannot hear very well, and it is dark inside the hive. As a result, they touch each other and use their senses of touch and smell to communicate.

A scientist named Karl von Frisch studied honeybees. He saw that honeybees move back and forth in a kind of "dance" when they return to the hive. They dance in different ways to tell other honeybees where to find food. Frisch saw that honeybees dance in a circle to show that food is near. They dance in a figure eight (∞) and **wiggle** to show that food is far away. The other honeybees in the hive use their senses of smell and touch to learn the **location** of the food from the dancing bees.

▲ Honeybees get food and nectar from flowers.

---

nectar, a sweet liquid found inside flowers
wiggle, to move and shake the body
location, place

▲ Honeybees use touch and smell to communicate with each other.

DISCUSS

How are the dances of honeybees like a language?

Review and Practice

1. Tell a partner the main ideas you learned about elephants, owls, and honeybees. Use the headings and pictures on pages 156–159 to help you.
2. What facts do you remember about each animal? Explain.

COMPREHENSION

Write the sentences below in your notebook. Use the words in the box to complete the sentences.

smell	~~survive~~	vibrations	touch
avoid	predators	vision	nectar

1. Animals use their senses to ___survive___ in nature.
2. To survive, animals need to find food and _____ danger.
3. Owls have very good _____.
4. Mother elephants _____ new babies with their trunks to welcome them.
5. Scientists think that elephants can feel _____ with their feet.
6. Elephants breathe and _____ with their trunks.
7. _____ catch and eat other animals.
8. Honeybees tell one another where to find _____ by dancing.

160

Extension

SENSORY IMAGES

Poems often have sensory images. Poets use sensory images so readers can see, hear, taste, touch, or smell things as the poet does. Read this poem.

Wings

If I had wings
I would touch the fingertips of clouds
and glide on the wind's breath.

If I had wings
I would taste a chunk of the sun
as hot as peppered curry.

If I had wings
I would listen to the clouds of sheep bleat
that graze on the blue.

If I had wings
I would breathe deep and sniff
the scent of raindrops.

If I had wings
I would gaze at the people
who cling to the earth.

If I had wings
I would dream of
swimming the deserts
and walking the seas.

—Pie Corbett

What can you see, hear, touch, taste, and smell in the poem? Copy the chart. Complete it with a partner.

See	Hear	Touch	Taste	Smell
people who cling to the earth				

Connect to Writing

GRAMMAR

Adjectives

Adjectives describe nouns—people, places, and things.
Adjectives can come after the verb *be*.

			be	adjective
An	elephant		is	**gentle.**
A	lion		is	**dangerous.**

Adjectives usually come before nouns.

adjective noun · adjective noun
An owl has **large** eyes and **excellent** vision.

adjective noun
Friendly elephants touch each other with their trunks.

Do not add -*s* to adjectives that describe more than one noun.

Elephants have **long** tusks.

Practice

Use the words to make sentences in your notebook. Put
the adjectives in the right place.

Example: sounds / hear / low / elephants

Elephants hear low sounds.

1. live / animals / environments / in / specific
2. long / elephant / tusks / the / has
3. trunk / strong / is / its
4. dance / honeybees / different / in / ways
5. dangerous / lions / are
6. dark / is / hive / a / honeybee's

SKILLS FOR WRITING

Writing a Descriptive Paragraph

Use adjectives and sensory images when you write a **description**. Then your reader can see, hear, taste, smell, or feel what the person, place, or thing you are describing is like.

Read this description that Carlos wrote about his dog. Then answer the questions.

Carlos Salgeras

My Dog Blue

My dog Blue has a long body and short legs. Blue's skin is very loose. When you pull his skin gently, it stretches like a rubber band! His ears are very long. Sometimes they fall into his food. Then his ears smell like dog food! Blue makes a loud, strange sound when he drinks water, "Thuk-a-thuk-a-thuk-a-thuk!" When he wants to go for a walk, he howls, "Ah-h-o-o-o-o-w!" Blue has a big head and a long nose. His face is wrinkled, and his eyes are sad. I named him "Blue" because "blue" means sad. Blue looks sad, but he's a very funny dog!

1. Which adjectives describe what Blue looks like?

2. What sensory images does Carlos use? Which senses do they describe?

3. How do Carlos's words and images make you feel about Blue? Explain.

WRITING PRACTICE

Descriptive Paragraph

You will write a descriptive paragraph about an animal. You can describe a pet, an animal you have seen at the zoo, or any animal you like.

1. **Read** Reread "Animal Senses" on pages 156–159 and Carlos's description of his dog on page 163. What descriptive words and images do the writers use?

Writing Strategy: Sensory Details Chart

A sensory details chart can help you describe how things look, smell, sound, taste, and feel. Carlos used this chart to write his description.

What I See	What I Smell	What I Hear	What I Feel
long body, nose, ears short legs big head, wrinkled face, sad eye	dog food on his ears	"Thuk-a-thuk-a-thuk-a-thuk!" when he drinks water "Ah-h-o-o-o-o-w!" when he howls	his loose skin stretches like a rubber band

---

2. **Make a chart** In your notebook, make a sensory details chart about your animal. Write words that describe what you see, smell, hear, and feel when you are near the animal.

3. **Write a descriptive paragraph** Use your chart to write a descriptive paragraph about your animal.

Link the Readings

Make a chart like the one below to compare the readings in this unit. Look at each word in the column. Put an **X** under "The Blind Men and the Elephant" if the word reminds you of the fable. Put an **X** under "Animal Senses" if the word reminds you of that selection. Put an **X** in both places if the word reminds you of both selections.

	"The Blind Men and the Elephant"	"Animal Senses"
trunk	_____	_____
vision	_____	_____
spear	_____	_____
communicate	_____	_____
prey	_____	_____
fan	_____	_____
snake	_____	_____

Check Your Knowledge

Language Development

1. What is a fable? How is it different from a legend?
2. What inferences did you make about the moral of "The Blind Men and the Elephant"?
3. What is a simile? Give an example of a simile and use it in a sentence.
4. What is an adjective? Give an example using an adjective and the verb *be*.

Science Content

1. What senses does an elephant use to survive?
2. How do owls use their sense of vision to hunt?
3. How do honeybees use their senses of touch and smell to communicate?

UNIT 7

The World of PLANTS

SELECTION 1 "Amazing Plants"

SELECTION 2 "Apollo and Daphne"

Plants give us food and oxygen. How do they do it? Find out when you read "Amazing Plants."

The myth "Apollo and Daphne" is an ancient Roman story. Read it to learn how the beautiful laurel tree came to be.

OBJECTIVES

Reading:
- **Vocabulary building:**
  Visual cues, dictionary skills
- **Reading strategies:**
  Use diagrams, visualize
- **Text types:**
  Science text, myth, drama

Writing:
- **Venn diagram**
- **Comparison**

Listening/Speaking:
- **Retell a myth**
- **Dramatize**
- **Sing**

Grammar:
- **Comparative form of adjectives**

Viewing/Representing:
- **Diagrams, charts, illustrations**

- **Science vocabulary**
- **Parts of a plant**
- **Photosynthesis**

167

Prepare to Read

"Amazing Plants" is a nonfiction science text. It tells how plants make their own food, make seeds, and help make new plants.

▲ Giant redwood trees

TRY TO PREDICT

1. How old do you think these trees are?
2. How do you think insects, birds, and other animals help plants?

▲ Hummingbird eating the sweet liquid inside a flower

LEARN KEY WORDS

absorb
oxygen
pollen
pollination
release
reproduce
roots
stem

VOCABULARY

Look at the pictures and the captions. They will help you learn the words in the box. Write the meaning of each word. Then check your work in a dictionary.

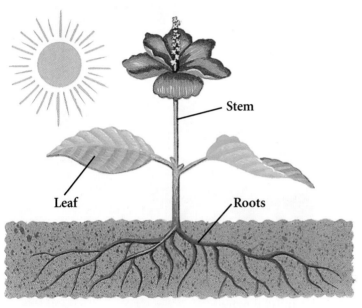

▲ The **roots** of a plant **absorb**, or take in, water from the ground. The **stem** holds up the plant. The leaves absorb sunlight and **release**, or give off, **oxygen** (OX-ih-jin), an important gas.

▲ During **pollination** (pol-ih-NAY-shun), bees carry **pollen** between many different flowers. Pollen, made of tiny grains, helps plants **reproduce**, or make seeds for new plants.

READING STRATEGY

Use Diagrams

The **diagrams**, or labeled drawings, in a science text give you important information.

- Look at each diagram carefully.
- Read all the labels.
- How does the diagram make ideas in the text clearer?

"Amazing Plants" is a nonfiction science text that tells about plants and how they grow. As you read, look carefully at the diagrams that go with the text.

Amazing Plants

Why Are Plants Amazing?

Plants are an amazing form of life. Scientists think there are about 300,000 different kinds of plants. Some plants are huge and old, like the giant redwood tree. Other plants, such as algae, are tiny and live in water. Some plants, like orchids, have beautiful flowers. Other plants, like the saguaro cactus, have sharp spines instead of leaves.

Without plants, most other forms of life on Earth could not live. Plants are an important food for many living things. People and many animals eat different parts of plants, including fruits, nuts, leafy vegetables, and seeds like grains. Plants also release oxygen into the air. People and animals need oxygen to live.

▲ Orchids have beautiful flowers.

▶ The saguaro cactus grows in the desert.

CHECK YOUR UNDERSTANDING

1. Give examples of two different kinds of plants.

2. Name two ways that plants are important to other living things.

▲ Apples are a major fruit crop in the United States.

Photosynthesis

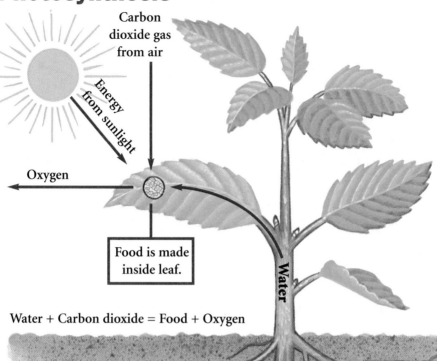

Carbon dioxide gas from air

Energy from sunlight

Oxygen

Food is made inside leaf.

Water

Water + Carbon dioxide = Food + Oxygen

▲ Plants make their own food through a process called photosynthesis.

▲ Photosynthesis happens in the leaves of plants.

How Do Plants Get Energy?

Living things need energy to grow and reproduce. People and animals get energy from food. Most plants get energy from sunlight. Plants use sunlight to make food. This process is called photosynthesis (foe-toe-SIN-thih-sis). In Greek, *photo* means "light" and *synthesis* means "put together," or "combine."

Photosynthesis happens in the leaves of plants. In photosynthesis, sunlight provides the energy needed to combine water with carbon dioxide gas from the air. This process makes food for the plant. It also releases oxygen into the air, as shown in the diagram above.

CHECK YOUR UNDERSTANDING

What happens in the process of photosynthesis?

What Does Each Part of a Plant Do?

The roots, the stem, and the leaves help a plant grow. Roots hold the plant in the ground. They support the plant under the ground. Hairs on the roots absorb water and minerals. Some roots—like carrots and potatoes—also store food.

The stem supports the plant above the ground. The stem connects the roots to the leaves. Tubes inside the stem carry water and minerals to the leaves.

Leaves absorb sunlight, which is the start of photosynthesis, the process of making food.

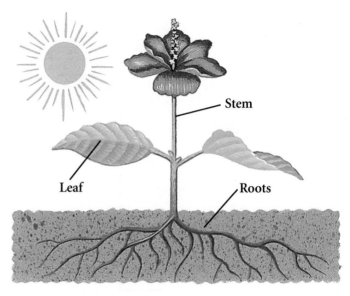

▲ Parts of a plant

How Do Flowers Help a Plant?

Flowers help a plant reproduce, or make new plants. Some plants have big, colorful flowers. The color and sweet smell attract insects, birds, and other animals. When insects and animals touch a flower, they often touch the pollen inside the flower. The pollen sticks to their bodies. Then, when the insect or animal moves to another flower, the pollen passes to that flower. This process is called pollination.

MAKE CONNECTIONS

What flowers grow in your home country?

◄ Butterflies pass pollen from flower to flower in a process called pollination.

How Does a Fruit Form?

When pollen reaches the **ovary** in the center of the flower, the plant can reproduce. Parts of the pollen and ovary combine, and the ovary grows larger. It becomes a fruit with seeds inside. The fruit protects the seeds as they grow. The seeds will later become new plants. Some fruits, such as peaches, have only one large seed inside. Others, like lemons, have many seeds.

▲ A peach has one large seed.

What Is the Plant Life Cycle?

When seeds fall to the ground, they begin a new **cycle** of plant life. Rain makes the seeds soft, and roots start to grow out of the seed and into the ground. New leaves and stems form and grow above the ground. The plants produce flowers. Insects pollinate the flowers, and seeds form again. This process is called the plant life cycle. The plant life cycle is one of many cycles in nature.

▲ A lemon has many small seeds.

---

ovary, place inside a flower where fruit and seeds form
cycle, events that happen again and again in the same order

PLANT LIFE CYCLE

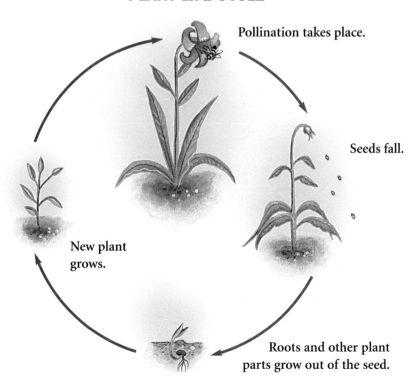

Pollination takes place.

Seeds fall.

New plant grows.

Roots and other plant parts grow out of the seed.

◀ Each event in the life cycle of flowering plants happens in the same order, year after year.

CHECK YOUR UNDERSTANDING

1. What happens in a plant after pollination?

2. Explain the plant life cycle.

173

Review and Practice

RETELL AND REVIEW

1. Tell a partner what you learned about plants. Use the headings and the pictures on pages 170–173 to help you.
2. How did the diagrams and labels help you understand the text?
3. Explain the diagram of photosynthesis on page 171.

COMPREHENSION

Write the sentences below in your notebook. Write *Yes* if the statement is true. Write *No* if it is not true. Then rewrite the statement correctly. Reread pages 170–173 to check your answers.

1. Plants make their own food. *Yes*
2. Insects, birds, and other animals pass energy from flower to flower.
3. The hairs on plant roots absorb water and minerals.
4. The stem supports the plant under the ground.
5. Photosynthesis happens in the roots of a plant.
6. Flowers help a plant reproduce.
7. A seed begins to grow in a flower after pollination.
8. The plant life cycle is the only cycle in nature.

Extension

FOLK SONG

This is a folk song about planting rows of seeds. The rhythm of the song makes it a good work song. Read the words. Then listen and sing along with the music.

Garden Song

Chorus

Inch by inch, row by row, gonna make this garden grow
All it takes is a rake and a hoe and a piece of **fertile** ground
Inch by inch, row by row, someone **bless** these seeds I **sow**
Someone warm them from below
'Till the rain comes tumbling down.

Pulling weeds and pickin' stones;
We are made of dreams and bones
I feel the need to grow my own 'cause the time is close at hand.
Grain for grain, sun and rain, I'll find my way in nature's chain
Tune my body and my brain to the music of the land.

Chorus

Plant your rows straight and long,
Temper them with prayer and song.
Mother Earth will keep you strong if you give her love and care.
An old crow watching hungrily from his **perch** in **yonder** tree.
In my garden I'm as free as that feathered thief up there.

Chorus

—David Mallett

fertile, able to grow a lot of plants
bless, say a prayer for
sow, place in the ground
temper, help, give treatment to
perch, branch, place where a bird stands
yonder, over there

Prepare to Read

"Apollo and Daphne" is an ancient Roman myth. In ancient times, people made up myths, or stories, to try to explain things in nature. This myth explains how the laurel tree came to be.

TRY TO PREDICT

1. What kind of arrow do you think the boy is shooting?
2. Why do you think the girl is running?

LEARN KEY WORDS

arrows
bark
bow
crowns
forest

VOCABULARY

Look at the pictures and the captions. They will help you learn the words in the box. Write the meaning of each word. Then check your work in a dictionary.

▲ Cupid played with his **bow** and **arrows**.

▲ Winning athletes sometimes wear **crowns** of laurel leaves.

◀ Many trees grow in a **forest**. Trees are covered with **bark**.

READING STRATEGY

Visualize

To **visualize** means to picture people, places, or things in your mind. Visualizing helps you understand the events in a story.

- As you read, look for words that describe the characters.
- Look for details about the story's setting (time and place).
- Look for words and details that describe events and actions.

Myths come from many different cultures. "Apollo and Daphne" started as a Greek myth. Then the Romans changed it a little. As you read, visualize the people, places, and events.

Apollo and Daphne

One day, Cupid, the young god of love, was playing with his little bow and arrows. The arrows were a gift from his mother, Venus. She was the goddess of love and beauty. Cupid's arrows were small, but they were powerful. They could make people fall in love.

Cupid wanted to be a hunter like Apollo, his uncle. However, Apollo didn't think Cupid was big and strong enough. One day, Apollo saw Cupid playing with his bow and arrows. "Put away your little arrows, Cupid," he said. "You can't be a hunter. You need to be bigger and stronger."

Apollo's words made Cupid angry. "You and your arrows are bigger," Cupid said, "but my arrows are more powerful." Cupid shot one of his arrows at Apollo and hit him. Cupid's arrow made Apollo fall in love with Daphne, the daughter of the river god, Peneus (puh-NEE-us).

CHECK YOUR UNDERSTANDING

What did Cupid's arrow do to Apollo?

Daphne was very beautiful. She had long hair and fair skin. Daphne was also very shy. She did not like talking to people, so she lived alone in the forest.

As soon as Apollo saw Daphne in the forest, he fell in love with her. He wanted to talk to her, so he followed her. Daphne was afraid and ran away from Apollo. She did not love him.

Apollo ran after her. "Daphne! Please, wait!" Apollo cried. "I love you. I am not your enemy." But Daphne did not stop. She ran farther into the forest.

They ran and ran. Daphne was fast, but Apollo was faster. Soon Daphne was tired, and Apollo came closer. Daphne called to her father, Peneus. "Father! I'm tired! You must help me!" The river god heard his daughter's voice.

"Don't worry, Daphne," he cried. "I am here. I will help you!"

MAKE CONNECTIONS

1. Are there forests in your home country? Explain.
2. Do you know any myths? Talk about them.

Suddenly, Daphne began to change. Her feet became roots, and they grew into the earth. Her arms became branches, and her hair became leaves. Daphne's body became covered in bark. She was now a beautiful laurel tree.

Apollo was amazed. He touched her branches and leaves. "You cannot be my wife," Apollo said sadly, "but you will always be my special tree. I will wear your leaves as my crown forever."

From that day, Apollo gave laurel crowns to all the great musicians, poets, and athletes in honor of Daphne, his one great love.

Even in our time, we still give laurel crowns to honor great athletes.

MAKE CONNECTIONS

1 Have you ever seen a picture of a laurel crown? Where?

2 What other ways do we honor great athletes or artists today?

Apollo and Daphne
A Play

Now read the same myth as a play. There are seven parts.

CHARACTERS

Narrator	**Daphne**
Venus	**Peneus**
Cupid	**Chorus**
Apollo	

Narrator: One day, Cupid was playing with his little bow and arrows. They were a gift from his mother, Venus. She was the goddess of love and beauty.

Venus: Be careful, Cupid. Those are special love arrows. They're very powerful.

Cupid (*aiming his bow and arrow*): I want to be a hunter like Uncle Apollo.

Apollo (*laughing*): You can't be a hunter, Cupid. You're too small. You need to be bigger and stronger.

Cupid (*angrily*): Your arrows are bigger than mine, Uncle Apollo. But my arrows are more powerful!

Chorus: Cupid shot one of his arrows and hit Apollo.

Venus: Oh, no! Now Apollo will fall in love.

Narrator: Apollo was walking in the forest. Suddenly, he saw a beautiful young woman.

Apollo: It's Daphne, daughter of Peneus. She is very beautiful.

Chorus: Apollo wanted to talk to Daphne. He followed her.

Daphne: Go away, Apollo! Don't follow me.

Narrator: Daphne was afraid, and she ran away.

Apollo: Daphne! Please, wait! I love you. I am not your enemy.

Chorus: They ran and ran. Daphne was fast, but Apollo was faster.

Daphne: Father! I'm tired! You must help me!

Peneus: Don't worry, Daphne. I'm here. I will help you!

Narrator: Suddenly, Daphne began to change.

Chorus: Her feet became roots. Her arms became branches, and her hair became leaves.

Narrator: Daphne's body became covered in bark.

Chorus: She had become a beautiful laurel tree!

Apollo: You will always be my special tree. I will wear your leaves as my crown forever.

Narrator: From that day forward, Apollo always wore a crown of laurel leaves. And he gave crowns of laurel leaves to all the great musicians, poets, and athletes.

Review and Practice

1. Look back at the pictures in "Apollo and Daphne" on pages 178–180. Cover the words on each page. Retell the events of the story to a partner, using only the pictures.

2. Did you visualize the myth the way the artist who drew the pictures did? Explain.

3. Draw a picture that shows how you visualized Daphne turning into a tree.

COMPREHENSION

Complete the sentences. Choose the correct word from the column on the right. Write the completed sentences in your notebook.

1. Cupid was playing with his bow and _arrows_ .   Peneus

2. Venus was the goddess of love and _____.   athletes

3. Cupid shot an arrow at _____.   river god

4. Daphne was the daughter of _____.   laurel tree

5. When Apollo called out to Daphne, she _____.   ~~arrows~~

6. Daphne's father was the _____.   Apollo

7. Suddenly, Daphne began to change into a _____.   ran away

8. Apollo gave laurel crowns to great musicians,   beauty
   poets, and _____.

Extension

SONG

Scientists think that an ancient redwood tree in California is about 12,000 years old! This song tells about some events in history that happened during the life of this amazing tree.

Giant Silent Redwood

Chorus

Giant Silent Redwood tell me what you know
Giant Silent Redwood tell me what you know
Stand and tell me what you know

Antony and Cleopatra kissed upon the Nile
You stood there Giant Redwood,
Tell me, did they smile?
Tell me, did they smile?

Chorus

Marco Polo walked to China, worked for
    Kublai Khan
You stood there Giant Redwood
Tell me how to move on
Tell me how to move on

Chorus

By, of, and for the people, Lincoln made
    a speech
You stood there Giant Redwood
Tell me how to teach
Tell me how to teach

Chorus

Loggers in the woods got their eye on you
You stand yet Giant Redwood
Tell me what to do
Tell me what to do
You stand yet Giant Redwood
Tell me what to do
Tell me what to do

—Dan Scanlan

Connect to Writing

GRAMMAR

The Comparative Form of Adjectives

Use the **comparative form** of an adjective to compare two people, places, or things.

For most one-syllable adjectives, add -er + than.

adjective	comparative
Cupid was **young**.	Cupid was **younger than** Apollo.
Daphne was **fast**.	Apollo was **faster than** Daphne.

For two-syllable adjectives that end in -y, change the y to i and add -er + than.

adjective	comparative
Cupid was **angry**.	Cupid was **angrier than** Apollo.

For most adjectives with two or more syllables, use more + adjective + than.

Cupid's arrows were **more powerful than** Apollo's.

Daphne was **more tired than** Apollo.

Practice

Copy these sentences in your notebook. Complete each sentence with the comparative form of the adjective in parentheses.

1. Cupid's arrows were _____smaller_____ than Apollo's. (small)

2. Venus was _____ than Daphne. (beautiful)

3. Apollo was _____ than Cupid. (strong)

4. Lions are _____ than elephants. (dangerous)

5. My Spanish homework is _____ than my English homework. (easy)

6. A peach seed is _____ than a lemon seed. (large)

7. Apollo was _____ than Peneus. (famous)

8. My science class is _____ than my social studies class. (difficult)

SKILLS FOR WRITING

Writing a Comparison

A comparison tells how two people, places, or things are alike and different. In a two-paragraph comparison, explain how the things are alike in the first paragraph. Then tell how they are different in the second paragraph. Use the word *both* to show how the things are alike. Use the comparative form of adjectives to show how they are different.

Read this two-paragraph comparison. Then answer the questions.

Eddie Monroy

Two Amazing Plants

A giant redwood and a saguaro cactus are alike in some ways. They both grow in the United States. Both are very tall plants. Both plants live to be very old. A redwood can live more than 3,000 years, and a saguaro can live to be 200 years old.

The giant redwood and the saguaro cactus are also different in many ways. The giant redwood grows taller and lives longer than the saguaro cactus. The giant redwood is covered with strong bark. The saguaro cactus is covered with sharp spines. The giant redwood needs a lot of rain and fog. The saguaro cactus needs little rain and lots of sun.

1. What two things does the writer compare?
2. What does the writer explain in the first paragraph? In the second paragraph?
3. What comparative forms does the writer use? What do they show?

WRITING PRACTICE

Comparison

You will write a two-paragraph comparison of two plants.

1. Read Reread the comparison on page 185. How does the writer show that the two kinds of plants are alike and different?

Writing Strategy: Venn Diagram

A Venn diagram shows how two things are alike and different. Eddie made this Venn diagram to compare a giant redwood and a saguaro cactus. The middle of his diagram shows how both plants are alike. The left and right parts of his diagram show how the plants are different.

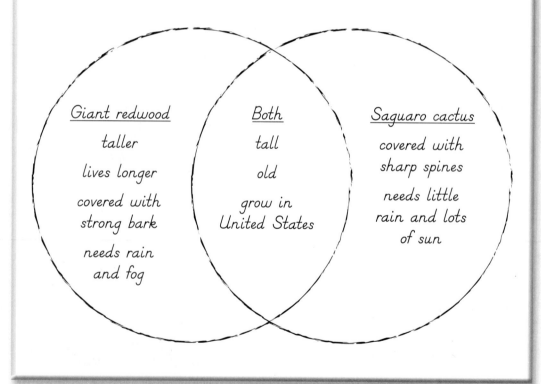

Giant redwood
taller
lives longer
covered with strong bark
needs rain and fog

Both
tall
old
grow in United States

Saguaro cactus
covered with sharp spines
needs little rain and lots of sun

2. Make a Venn diagram Draw a Venn diagram in your notebook. List ways your two plants are alike and different.

3. Write Use your Venn diagram to write two paragraphs comparing your plants. In the first paragraph, explain how the plants are alike. In the second paragraph, tell how they are different.

186

Link the Readings

Make a chart like the one below to compare the readings in this unit. Look at each word in the column. Put an **X** under "Amazing Plants" if the word reminds you of that selection. Put an **X** under "Apollo and Daphne" if the word reminds you of the myth. Put an **X** in both places if the word reminds you of both selections.

	"Amazing Plants"	"Apollo and Daphne"
fiction	_____	_____
nonfiction	_____	_____
photosynthesis	_____	_____
roots and leaves	_____	_____
laurel tree	_____	_____
giant redwood	_____	_____
pollination	_____	_____

Check Your Knowledge

Language Development
1. How can diagrams help you understand a nonfiction text?
2. What does visualize mean?
3. What is the comparative form of the adjective *short*?
4. What is the comparative form of the adjective *dangerous*?

Science Content
1. Name three parts of a plant. What does each part do?
2. How do insects and animals help with pollination?
3. Why is photosynthesis important to a plant?
4. Explain what happens in the plant cycle.

WINGS

PART 1

 "Bessie Coleman, American Flyer"

"This Big Sky"

PART 2

"Aaron's Gift"

"Cher Ami—World War I Hero"

Since ancient times, people have wanted to fly and be free, like birds. People studied birds to find out how their wings worked. They used what they learned about flight to build flying machines. The invention of the airplane finally gave people wings of their own.

In Part 1, you will learn about Bessie Coleman. Bessie Coleman dreamed of flying and worked hard to make her dream come true. You will also read a poem about dreams and flying.

In Part 2, you will read a story about a boy who rescues a pigeon with a broken wing. Finally, you will read about a bird that saved the lives of American soldiers.

Prepare to Read

BACKGROUND

"Bessie Coleman, American Flyer" is a nonfiction text. It is a biography of Bessie Coleman, the first African-American woman to fly an airplane.

Make connections Bessie Coleman grew up in Texas in the early 1900s. At that time in the American South, African Americans were not free to live as they wished. Black people could not live in the same neighborhoods or go to the same schools as white people. They could not even eat in restaurants with white people. For Bessie Coleman, there was a way to escape her hard life and feel free. That way was to fly.

Look at the map and answer the questions.

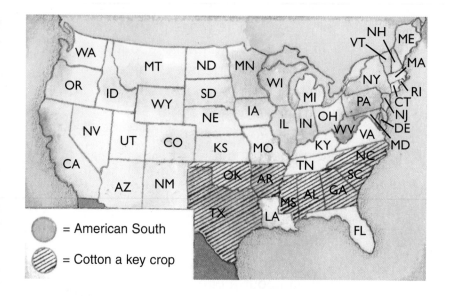

= American South

= Cotton a key crop

1. Which states are part of the American South?
2. In which states was cotton a key crop?

LEARN KEY WORDS

encouraged
famous
publisher
thrilling
toured

VOCABULARY

Look at the pictures and the captions. They will help you learn the words in the box. Write the meaning of each word. Then check your work in a dictionary.

◀ Robert Abbott was a newspaper **publisher**, or owner. He **encouraged** Bessie to go to France.

▲ Bessie **toured** the country in her plane. She did flying tricks and put on **thrilling**, or exciting, air shows.

◀ Bessie Coleman is **famous**. This U.S. postage stamp was made in her honor.

READING STRATEGY

Summarize

To **summarize** means to write the main ideas of a text in your own words.

- As you read, summarize each section.
- Keep your summaries simple.
- After you finish reading the text, reread your summaries. This will help you understand and remember the main ideas.

Social Studies

"Bessie Coleman, American Flyer" is a biography of the first African-American woman pilot. As you read, summarize each section.

BESSIE COLEMAN
AMERICAN FLYER

Bessie Coleman was the first African American to get an international pilot's **license**. She was also the first African-American woman to fly an airplane. Bessie was brave, smart, and determined to do something special with her life. She did not let **prejudice** stop her.

Bessie's Childhood

Bessie Coleman was born into a large family in Atlanta, Texas, on January 26, 1892. She grew up in a time of **discrimination**. In the South, African Americans couldn't go to school with white people. They couldn't eat at the same table or ride in the same train car. Life was very hard.

Bessie's parents were hard-working cotton farmers. They moved the family to the small city of Waxahachie, Texas. The whole family worked in the cotton fields at harvest time. When not helping out in the field, Bessie and her brothers and sisters went to a one-room schoolhouse for African-American children.

▲ Bessie Coleman

▼ Picking cotton at harvest time

---

license, a formal statement of your ability to do something
prejudice, an unfair dislike of someone who is of another race or religion
discrimination, treating one group of people in an unfair way

◀ An African-American schoolroom in the early 1900s

The school had few supplies. Sometimes there were not enough books, pencils, or paper to go around. But that didn't stop Bessie from walking four miles there and four miles back. Bessie loved school and was a great reader. She was also very good at math and soon became the family's bookkeeper. Bessie completed all eight grades at her school and wanted to learn more. She saved her money and went to an African-American college for one year. Then her money ran out, and she went back home to work.

The Beginning of a Dream

When she was twenty-three, Bessie moved to Chicago to live with her brother. She hoped to find a better life there. Soon her mother and three younger sisters moved to Chicago, too. Bessie loved the excitement of the big city. She watched the great musician Louis Armstrong and other talented African-American performers play jazz. Chicago was an exciting place to be.

Bessie soon got a job at a barber shop. There, she listened to men tell stories about World War I. Some of them had been pilots in France. Bessie decided that she wanted to become a pilot, too. But who would teach her? Flight schools were all-white and all-male. There were no African-American instructors then. Bessie had to find a way to make her dream come true.

▲ Chicago in the 1920s

BEFORE YOU GO ON . . .

1️⃣ How did Bessie Coleman spend her days as a child?

2️⃣ What was Bessie Coleman's dream?

HOW ABOUT YOU?

• Do you like small towns or big cities? Explain.

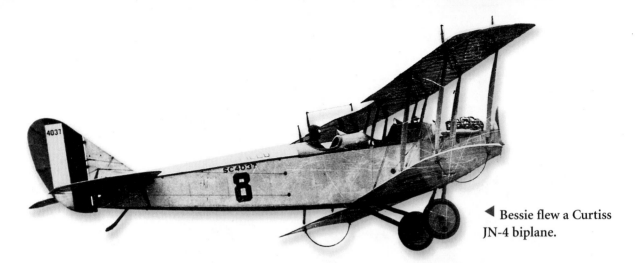

◀ Bessie flew a Curtiss JN-4 biplane.

Bessie's friend Robert Abbott was the publisher of the *Chicago Defender,* a newspaper that wrote about African Americans at a time when other papers did not. He encouraged Bessie to go to flight school in France. First, Bessie studied French. Then she sailed on a ship to France.

The flight training was difficult and dangerous. Sometimes the 27-foot **biplanes** they used had accidents, and some pilots were killed. But Bessie did not give up. On June 15, 1921, she received her international pilot's license. Bessie was finally a pilot!

Returning Home

Bessie returned to the United States in September 1921. Many newspaper reporters came to meet her. Bessie dressed like a pilot. She wore tall, shiny boots and a helmet with goggles. Large crowds watched her thrilling air shows.

Bessie became famous. She was the guest of honor at an African-American musical. The audience stood up and clapped and clapped for her. Bessie was proud of her own accomplishments, and she was proud to be an African American.

▲ Bessie in her pilot's uniform

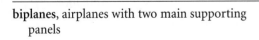

▲ Goggles protect a pilot's eyes.

---

biplanes, airplanes with two main supporting panels

Free to Fly

For the next five years, Bessie toured the country. Thousands of people came to watch her perform thrilling stunts at her air shows. Bessie encouraged other African Americans to fly. "The air is the only place free from prejudices," she said. Bessie wanted to start a flight school for African Americans. To gain support for the school, she traveled across the country to give flying shows.

Bessie practiced before each show. Her last performance—and her last flight—was on April 30, 1926. Her plane went into a **tailspin**, and Bessie fell to her death.

Bessie's body was brought home to Chicago. Many, many people went to her funeral. They wanted to honor the woman who had the courage to follow her dream.

▲ This newspaper cartoon celebrated Bessie's success as a pilot.

Bessie Remembered

Bessie Coleman's flying career was short, but her skill and love of flying are still remembered. She has **inspired** countless young African Americans to become pilots. Many flying clubs are named for her. A street in Chicago is now called Bessie Coleman Drive. In 1995, a U.S. postage stamp was made in her honor. Every spring, African-American pilots fly over "Brave Bessie's" grave in Chicago. They drop flowers on the grave in honor of the little girl with a big dream.

---

tailspin, an uncontrolled fall of a plane through the air
inspired, encouraged someone to do something good

BEFORE YOU GO ON . . .

1. Why was Bessie Coleman an unusual pilot?
2. Describe how people remember Bessie.

HOW ABOUT YOU?

- Bessie's dream was to become a pilot. What is your dream?

BLACK HERITAGE

USA 32 BESSIE COLEMAN

195

Review and Practice

The list of events below from "Bessie Coleman, American Flyer" are out of order. Reread the biography on pages 192–195. Copy the chart below in your notebook. Then put the events in their correct time order.

Events: Bessie got her pilot's license.
Bessie returned to the United States.
~~Bessie worked hard in school.~~
Bessie listened to Louis Armstrong and other Chicago jazz musicians.
Bessie went to France.
Bessie toured the country in air shows.

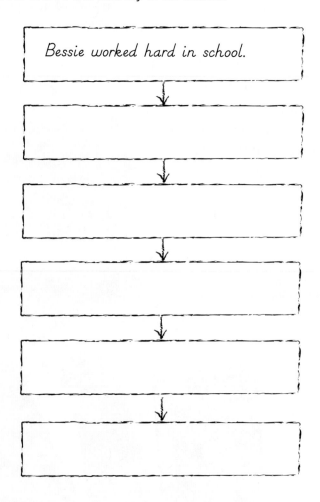

Bessie worked hard in school.

Compare charts with a partner.

EXTENSION

Find out about some other famous pilots. Examples include the Wright brothers, Charles Lindbergh, and Amelia Earhart. Use the following sources:

- biographies
- books about the history of aviation
- the Internet
- encyclopedias

Write a short report telling what you learned about the pilot. Share your report with your classmates.

DISCUSSION

Discuss in pairs or small groups.

1. Why do you think Bessie Coleman wanted to become a pilot?
2. Why was it difficult for her to become a pilot?
3. How did Bessie use her fame to help others?

CONNECT TO LITERATURE

Poem

THIS BIG SKY

This sky is big enough
for all my dreams.

Two **ravens** burst black
from a piñon tree
into the blare
of blazing sun.

I follow their wide **ebony** flight
over **copper** hills,
down canyons **shimmering** gold
autumn leaves.

Two ravens spread their wings, rise
into **whispers**
of giant **pines**, over mountains blue
with **memories**.

This sky is big enough
for all my dreams.

—**Pat Mora**

---

ravens, large black birds
ebony, black
copper, orange-brown
shimmering, shining and shaking
whispers, soft sounds
pines, trees with green needles
memories, things you remember

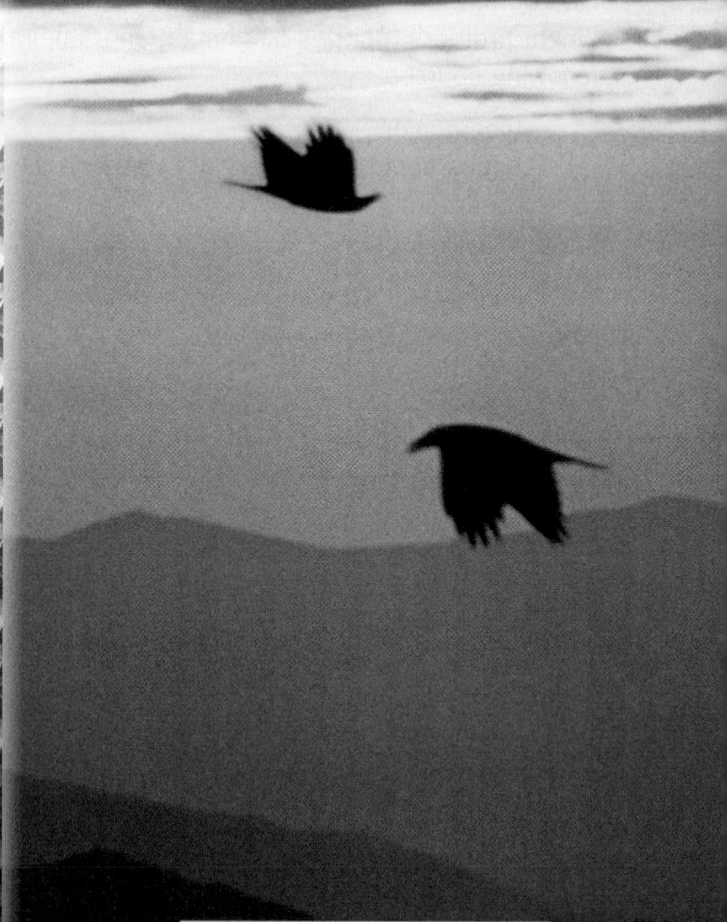

BEFORE YOU GO ON . . .

1. What did you visualize as you read the poem?
2. What idea is repeated in the poem?

HOW ABOUT YOU?

- How do you feel when you watch a bird flying? Explain.

Link the Readings

REFLECTION

Reread the selections on pages 192–195 and page 198. Then copy the chart in your notebook and complete it.

Title	Type of Text	What It's About	Main Idea
"Bessie Coleman, American Flyer"			
"This Big Sky"			

DISCUSSION

Discuss in pairs or small groups.

1. How are the ideas about flying alike in both selections?
2. Do you think Bessie Coleman would like the poem "This Big Sky"? Explain.
3. Have you ever flown in a plane? If so, tell about it.

Connect to Writing

GRAMMAR

Imperatives

Use **imperatives** to give instructions, directions, or orders. The subject of an imperative sentence is usually *you*. The subject is usually not stated.

subject	verb	
	Open your books to page 24.	
(You)	**Turn** right on Main Street.	
	Finish your homework.	

Use the word *please* to make an imperative more polite. *Please* can come at the beginning or the end of a sentence. Use a comma when *please* comes at the end.

Please eat your breakfast.
Wash the dishes, **please.**

Practice

Read the eight examples. In your notebook, write an imperative sentence for each example.

1. John wants Sam to stop talking. John should say:
Please stop talking, Sam.

2. It might rain, so Dana wants her daughter Angela to take an umbrella.
Dana should say:

3. Luke the dog is about to grab Molly's sandwich.
Molly should say:

4. Steve is at track practice. Paula wants to meet him afterward.
Paula should say:

5. Ahmed loves milk shakes. Ahmed's dad makes great milk shakes.
Ahmed should tell his dad:

6. Irina has a bad cold. Nicolo wants her to feel better.
Nicolo should say:

7. Lee wants her brother Tim to feed her bird.
Lee should say:

8. Jake can't answer the phone. His sister Sally is sitting right next to the phone. Jake should say:

SKILLS FOR WRITING

Writing Instructions

Instructions should be easy to understand. Here are some ways to write good instructions:

- Organize your instructions in numbered steps.
- Make sure that each step is simple and clear.
- If possible, include a diagram to show each step.
- Ask a classmate to read your instructions. Can he or she follow them easily?

How to Make a Paper Airplane, by Kevin Eng

1. Fold the paper in half. Open the paper and fold the top corners down.

2. Fold each side across the dotted lines to make wings.

3. Bring the wings together. Then fold each wing down along the dotted lines.

1. How are the instructions organized?
2. How does Kevin make the instructions simple and clear?
3. How do the diagrams make the instructions easier to understand?

WRITING PRACTICE

Instructions

You will write instructions that explain how to do or make something. Here are some ideas:

- how to make scrambled eggs
- how to make your bed
- how to send and receive e-mail
- how to wash and dry clothes
- how to teach a dog to catch a ball

1. **Read** Look back at the model on page 201. Are the instructions easy to understand?

Writing Strategy: Draw Diagrams

Diagrams can help make instructions easier to understand and follow. On page 201, Kevin's diagrams show what the paper airplane looks like as you do each step. The diagrams show information that Kevin does not need to include in his writing. You can use similar diagrams to make your instructions easier to understand.

---

2. **Draw diagrams** Draw a picture of each step of your instructions.

3. **Write** Write step-by-step instructions for the process you are going to describe. When you finish, reread your instructions. Are they clear? Are they easy to follow? Are they complete? Be sure you have included all the necessary information.

PART REVIEW 1

Check Your Knowledge

Language Development

1. How did summarizing the biography in Part 1 help you remember the main ideas?

2. Write an imperative sentence. What is the subject of your sentence?

3. What is a good way to organize instructions? How can drawing diagrams help make your instructions easier to understand?

Academic Content

1. What social studies words did you learn in Part 1? What do the words mean?

2. Who was Bessie Coleman?

3. How did Bessie Coleman inspire other people?

4. What visual images do you remember from the poem "This Big Sky"? Explain.

PART 2 Prepare to Read

OBJECTIVES

LANGUAGE DEVELOPMENT

Reading:
- Vocabulary building: *Visual cues, dictionary skills*
- Reading strategy: *Understand an author's purpose*
- Text types: *Short story, social studies text*

Writing:
- Outline
- Review

Listening/Speaking:
- Retell a story
- Discussion

Grammar:
- Subject-verb agreement

Viewing/Representing:
- Charts, photos, illustrations, maps

ACADEMIC CONTENT
- Social studies vocabulary
- World War I
- Eastern European history

BACKGROUND

"Aaron's Gift" is a short story. It takes place in New York City in the 1940s. The main character is a boy named Aaron, who lives with his parents and grandmother. In the story, Aaron remembers his grandmother's story about something that happened to her as a girl in Ukraine. When the story was written, Ukraine was called "the Ukraine." In the early 1900s, soldiers called Cossacks persecuted Jewish people in Russia and Ukraine—they treated them cruelly because of their religious beliefs. Cossacks sometimes destroyed villages and killed many people. Over time, many Jews left Ukraine and Russia and came to the United States.

Make connections Aaron's grandmother lived through a Cossack attack as a young girl. In the story, Aaron uses the name "Cossacks" to describe some boys who are cruel.

Look at the map and answer the questions.

1. Is Ukraine east or west of the major part of Russia?
2. What three countries are south of Russia?

LEARN KEY WORDS

broken
grabbed
leaped
soothe
wounded

VOCABULARY

Look at the pictures and the captions. They will help you learn the words in the box. Write the meaning of each word. Then check your work in a dictionary.

▲ The **wounded** pigeon did not move. Its left wing was **broken**.

▲ Aaron gently picked up the bird and tried to **soothe**, or comfort, it.

▲ Aaron **leaped** up and **grabbed** the bird with his hands.

READING STRATEGY

Understand an Author's Purpose

Authors write fiction for different purposes, or reasons. For example, sometimes an **author's purpose** is to entertain the reader. Sometimes his or her purpose is to teach the reader something. An author may have more than one purpose for writing.

- As you read, think about the author's purpose for writing the story.

- Write down words and details that show the author's purpose.

- Reread the story. Do you think the author had one—or more than one—purpose?

FOCUS ON LITERATURE

Short Story

"Aaron's Gift" is a short story about a boy who finds a hurt pigeon. By helping the bird, he learns an important lesson. As you read, think about the author's purpose for writing this story.

Aaron's Gift

Adapted from the story by Myron Levoy

Aaron went to Tompkins Square Park to roller-skate because the streets around his house were too crowded with children and dogs and traffic. He skated back and forth, pretending he was in a race. Then he noticed a pigeon on the grass.

The pigeon looked hurt. It tried to fly, but its left wing wouldn't flap. Aaron thought the wing looked broken. He took a cookie from his pocket and tossed some crumbs on the ground. "Here pidge, here pidge," he said.

The pigeon strutted over to eat the crumbs. Aaron pulled off his shirt. Moving slowly, he covered the wounded pigeon with his shirt and captured it. "Good pidge," he said softly. "That's your new name. Pidge."

The pigeon **struggled**. Aaron stroked the bird and tried to soothe it. "I'm going to take you home, Pidge," he said. "I'm going to fix you up. Easy, Pidge."

---

struggled, moved wildly

Aaron skated out of the park and headed for home. He held the pigeon in his hands. When he reached his house, he saw his friend Noreen on the stoop. "Is he sick?" asked Noreen.

"Broken wing," Aaron responded. "I'm going to fix it. Want to help?"

"Yes, I'll help," said Noreen.

Aaron and Noreen began to fix the pigeon's wing. They used two ice-cream sticks and strips of cloth to hold the wing in place. Pidge did not move while the children fixed his broken wing. He seemed to know they were trying to help him.

Aaron wasn't sure what his mother would say about his new pet. But he knew his grandmother would be happy for him.

She liked to feed crumbs to the birds on the back fire escape. Sometimes Aaron heard her talking to the birds about her childhood in the Ukraine. Aaron knew she would love Pidge.

To his surprise, Aaron's mother told him he could keep Pidge temporarily. That meant he could keep Pidge for a while. But when Aaron's father came home, he stared at the pigeon with the bandaged wing. "Who did this?" he asked.

"Me," said Aaron. "And Noreen."

"You're a genius!" his father said. "You're only a kid and you fixed a bird's wing. Just like a real doctor." Aaron could tell that his father would let him keep Pidge.

BEFORE YOU GO ON . . .

1. What was wrong with the pigeon?
2. How did Aaron help the pigeon?

HOW ABOUT YOU?

● Did you ever find an animal that was hurt? Explain what happened.

Aaron decided to train Pidge to be a **carrier pigeon**. He tied a little cardboard tube to Pidge's left leg. Inside the tube he put secret messages. Then he had Pidge walk across the living room toward a pile of crumbs. "When your wing is stronger," Aaron told Pidge, "you can fly with messages like a real carrier pigeon."

Aaron told all his friends about Pidge. Soon the whole neighborhood was talking about him. But it was a mistake to let everyone know about Pidge. A gang of older boys lived in the neighborhood. They had their own clubhouse. Aaron wanted to join the gang more than anything else. He wanted to learn their secret words. He wanted to belong. Carl, the gang leader, said Aaron could be a member if he brought Pidge to the clubhouse. Aaron couldn't believe it! He raced home to tell his mother.

But his mother didn't like the boys. She told Aaron to keep away from them. Then she asked him to make something special for Grandma's birthday. That way he would be too busy to think about the gang.

Aaron wanted to give Grandma something special for her birthday. He thought about what it could be. All at once, he knew. Pidge would be her present! Pidge could carry messages for her. Maybe Pidge could even make her feel better about something that happened a long time ago.

Aaron remembered the story Grandma had told him many times. When she was a little girl in the Ukraine, she had a pet goat. She loved the goat more than anything. Aaron thought she must have loved the goat as much as he loved Pidge.

---

carrier pigeon, a bird that is trained to
  carry messages

One day, the people in Grandma's village got some terrible news. They knew the **czar** hated all the Jewish people. Now, he had ordered his soldiers, the Cossacks, to attack their village. The Cossacks were coming! Grandma's family had to hide quickly in the cellar. Grandma had to leave her goat upstairs. If it made a sound, the soldiers would find their hiding place.

Soon Grandma and her family heard the sound of horses galloping into the village. Then the Cossacks were in their house, breaking furniture and smashing all of their things. Grandma thought the terrible noise would never end, but finally the house was quiet. The family came out of the cellar.

The first thing Grandma saw was her goat. It was on the floor, dead. Grandma was heartbroken. She cried for days for her lost pet. Aaron knew that even now, she was still sad about her goat. But maybe Pidge could somehow replace Grandma's long-lost pet. Wouldn't that be the best gift he could give her?

Aaron was excited that he had thought of just the right present for Grandma. But he hadn't forgotten about wanting to join the gang. A few days later, he met Carl in the street again. "Bring the pigeon to our clubhouse," Carl said. "We've got a new kind of **badge** for you. A membership badge."

---

badge, a small piece of paper, plastic, or fabric that shows you belong to a special group

czar, a Russian ruler before 1917

BEFORE YOU GO ON . . .

1 Why did Aaron want to join the gang of older boys?

2 What happened to Grandma's goat?

HOW ABOUT YOU?
- Did you ever want to join a club or a special group?

Aaron raced home to get Pidge. Gently, he removed the strips of cloth and the sticks. Pidge's wing seemed to be completely healed. With Pidge in his arms, Aaron ran to the clubhouse. Carl came out. "Give me the bird," he said.

"Be careful," Aaron warned. "I just took the bandages off."

"Oh sure, don't worry," said Carl. Then he turned to one of the other club members. "Give Aaron his special badge," Carl said. "And light the fire."

"What fire?" Aaron asked.

"Hey!" said Carl. "Don't ask questions. I'm the leader here. Now light the fire, Al."

The boy named Al struck a match. Soon the fire was glowing with a bright yellow-orange flame.

"Get the rope," Carl said. Another boy brought a rope, and Carl tied it around the bird.

"What . . . what are you doing?" shouted Aaron. "You're hurting his wing!"

"Don't worry about his wing," said Carl. "We're going to throw him into the fire, and you're going to pledge an oath to—"

"No!" shouted Aaron.

"Grab him!" Carl said to the other boys.

Aaron acted quickly. He leaped across the fire at Carl and **punched** him in the face. Carl slid to the floor and dropped Pidge. Aaron grabbed Pidge and raced out of the clubhouse. But before he could get very far, the boys were on top of him. He fell to the ground. Pidge slipped out of his hands. The rope came loose from around the bird's wings, and Pidge flew away.

At that moment Aaron hated the gang more than he had ever hated anyone in his life. He thought of the worst, the most terrible thing he could shout at them. "Cossacks!" he screamed. "You're all Cossacks!" Then he broke away and started running.

---

punched, hit with fists

When Aaron got home, his parents and Grandma saw his bloody face and torn shirt. "What happened?" they asked. **Sobbing**, Aaron told them about the gang, the clubhouse, and the fire. He told them how he had planned to give Pidge to Grandma as a gift. He told them how he thought Pidge was the best present he could ever give her.

Aaron's grandmother looked lovingly at her grandson. Then she kissed him and thanked him for his present. Aaron didn't understand. What was she talking about? Pidge was gone. Aaron didn't have any present for Grandma at all.

---

sobbing, crying with short, quick breaths

Later that night, before he fell asleep, Aaron thought about Pidge. He knew Grandma would have loved Pidge. She would have loved talking to him and taking care of him. But then Aaron realized something else. Grandma would have loved Pidge so much that she would have wanted Pidge to be free. She would have let Pidge go.

And then Aaron knew what Grandma meant when she thanked him for her present. Pidge's freedom was the best gift she could have had. For her, it was as if her goat had escaped from the Cossacks. It was as if her goat were free. Then Aaron fell asleep with a smile on his face.

BEFORE YOU GO ON . . .

1 Why did Carl want Pidge?

2 Why was Grandma happy at the end?

HOW ABOUT YOU?

- Have you ever given someone a special gift? Describe how it made you feel.

Review and Practice

The characters in the story "Aaron's Gift" face many problems. Each problem has its own solution. Read the sentences in the boxes below. Then write a solution for each problem.

Problem	Solution
The bird has a broken wing.	*Aaron fixes it using ice-cream sticks.*
Aaron wants to train Pidge to be a carrier pigeon.	
Aaron wants to join the gang.	
Aaron needs a gift for Grandma.	
Carl tries to hurt Pidge.	
Pidge flies away. Aaron has no gift for Grandma.	

Use your finished chart to retell the events of the story.

EXTENSION

What should you do if you find a hurt animal? To find out, contact or
go to one or more of the following sources for information.

- park ranger
- library
- nature center
- animal shelter
- zoo
- Internet

Use the information you find to make a poster that tells how a park
ranger or other adult would treat an injured animal.

DISCUSSION

Discuss in pairs or small groups.

1. How did Aaron's mother feel about Carl's club? Was she right about the club? Explain.
2. Why did Aaron think that Pidge would be a good gift for Grandma?
3. Why was Aaron's grandmother happy even though Aaron had no gift for her?
4. Why did Aaron call the gang of boys "Cossacks"?

Social Studies

In this nonfiction text, you will read about a special pigeon named Cher Ami. In French, cher ami *means "dear friend." Look at the pictures. Why do you think Cher Ami was special?*

Cher Ami—World War I Hero

During World War I (1914–1918), American soldiers used radios to talk to each other. The radios often broke. Carrier pigeons were another way for soldiers to communicate. Soldiers put a message in a small metal tube. They tied it to the leg of a pigeon. Then the pigeon carried the message to soldiers in another place.

Cher Ami was a famous carrier pigeon in World War I. He carried twelve messages in France. His last message saved many American soldiers. In 1918, enemy German soldiers **surrounded** a **battalion** of American soldiers. The battalion's radio broke. Later, another group of American soldiers thought the battalion was German and started shooting at them. German *and* American soldiers were attacking the battalion!

The battalion had three carrier pigeons. Two pigeons flew with messages to the American soldiers. German soldiers shot them. Cher Ami was the last pigeon. He was shot in the chest and leg, but he carried a message to the American soldiers. The shooting stopped, and 194 soldiers in the battalion were saved.

The French government gave Cher Ami a medal of honor. He was a hero.

▲ Cher Ami

BEFORE YOU GO ON . . .

1 How did soldiers use carrier pigeons in World War I?

2 How did Cher Ami save soldiers' lives?

HOW ABOUT YOU?
- Can other animals be heroes? Explain.

---

surrounded, were all around
battalion, a large group of soldiers

Link the Readings

Reread the story on pages 206–211 and the selection on page 214. Then copy the chart in your notebook and complete it.

Title	Type of Text	What It's About	Main Idea
"Aaron's Gift"			
"Cher Ami—World War I Hero"			

DISCUSSION

Discuss in pairs or small groups.

1. How are Pidge and Cher Ami alike? How are they different?
2. Do you think soldiers use carrier pigeons today? Why or why not?
3. Have you ever had a pet that was special to you? Explain.

KEEP HIM FREE

W.S.S.
WAR SAVINGS STAMPS
ISSUED BY THE
UNITED STATES
GOVERNMENT

BUY WAR SAVINGS STAMPS
ISSUED BY THE UNITED STATES TREASURY DEPT.

Connect to Writing

GRAMMAR

Subject-Verb Agreement: Simple Present

In the simple present, the subject and the verb of a sentence must agree.
When the subject is a singular noun or *he, she,* or *it,* add *-s* or *-es* to the verb.
When a verb ends in *-y,* change the *y* to *i* and add *-es.*

> **Aaron finds** a pigeon in the park.
> **He fixes** the pigeon's wing with Noreen.
> **She helps** him.
> **The pigeon carries** messages.

When the subject is a plural noun or *I, you, we,* or *they,* use the base form of the verb. Do not add *-s* or *-es.*

> **We have** a clubhouse.
> **You read** every night.
> **Carrier pigeons help** people communicate.

Practice

Copy the sentences in your notebook. Choose the correct subject or verb.

1. Mike (find/finds) a baby bird.
2. The cars (move/moves) slowly along the highway.
3. The (dog/dogs) catches the ball.
4. (He/They) listen carefully to the teacher.
5. The monkey (eat/eats) fruit.
6. (Plant/Plants) need water and sunlight.

SKILLS FOR WRITING

Writing a Review

A review gives the writer's opinion about a book, a story, a movie, or a show. A review includes:

- information about the work: the title, the author, what the work is about
- the writer's opinion: how he or she feels about the work
- reasons and examples that support the writer's opinion
- the writer's recommendation: advice about whether or not to see or read the work

Read the review. Then discuss the questions below.

Shonna Reese

"Aaron's Gift"

The story "Aaron's Gift" by Myron Levoy is very exciting. It's about a boy named Aaron who finds a pigeon with a broken wing. He calls the bird "Pidge" and fixes its wing. Aaron decides to give Pidge to his grandma for her birthday. When Grandma was a child in Ukraine, she had a pet goat. But the Cossacks killed it, and Grandma was very sad. Aaron thinks she will be happy to have a pet again. But Aaron also wants to join a gang of boys. The boys want Pidge, too. I can't tell you what happens because it would spoil the ending. All I can say is I really liked the story. It seemed like real life. I think you should read "Aaron's Gift."

1. How does the writer feel about the story?
2. What details does she give about the story?
3. What advice does she give her readers?

WRITING PRACTICE

Review

You will write a review of a favorite book, story, movie, or show.

1. **Read** Reread the model on page 217. What kind of work would you like to review? Make a list of ideas.

2. **Make a chart** To write her review, Shonna used the outline below. In your notebook, make an outline to organize your ideas for the review you are going to write.

Writing Strategy: Outline
Shonna organized her review around three main topics. Then she listed details to support each main idea.

> I. Introduction
>   A. Title, author, and description
>   B. Opinion
> II. The story
>   A. Characters: Aaron, Pidge, Grandma, and gang
>   B. Plot
>   1. Aaron fixes Pidge's broken wing.
>   2. Aaron wants to give Pidge to Grandma.
>   3. The gang wants Pidge, too.
> III. My recommendation: You should read this story.

3. **Write** Use your outline as a guide when you write your review.

Check Your Knowledge

Language Development

1. What was the author's purpose for writing "Aaron's Gift"? What details and words helped you to understand his purpose?

2. What lesson does Aaron learn at the end of the story?

3. Write a sentence in the simple present with *I*, *we*, or *they* as the subject. Write the same sentence with *he*, *she*, or *it* as the subject. How does the verb for the second sentence change?

4. What is a review? What does it include?

Academic Content

1. What new social studies vocabulary did you learn in Part 2? What do the words mean?

2. What terrible thing happened to Aaron's grandmother when she was a little girl in Ukraine? Explain.

3. What connection do you see between flight and freedom? How do the selections in Part 1 and Part 2 show this connection?

Put It All Together

OBJECTIVES

Integrate Skills
- Listening/
  Speaking:
  Tell a story
- Writing:
  Short story

Investigate Themes
- Projects
- Further
  reading

TELL A STORY

You will tell a story about a person who had a problem and found a solution.

1 **Think about it** Think about people you know or have read about who had a problem and solved it. Choose one person to write about. You could also write about a character you create.

Make an idea map. First, draw a circle and write the person's name inside it. Next, draw lines coming out of the circle. On one line, write the problem the person had. On another line, write how the person solved it. Write details about the person and the problem on the other lines.

2 **Organize** A story has a beginning, middle, and end. Use your idea map to make note cards for your story.

- *On card 1:* Write one or two facts to describe the person. This is the beginning of your story.

- *On card 2:* Write the problem he or she had. This is the middle of your story.

- *On card 3:* Write how he or she solved the problem. This is the end of your story.

- You may wish to use pictures to help you tell your story. If so, find or draw them.

SPEAKING TIPS

- Speak loudly and clearly.
- Look at the people you are talking to.

LISTENING TIPS

- Look at the speaker as he or she tells the story.
- If you have a question, write it down and wait until the speaker is finished to ask it.

3 **Practice** Use your note cards to practice telling your story. Then, put the cards away and tell your story from memory.

4 **Present and evaluate** Tell your story to the group. When each person finishes, evaluate the story. What did you like about it? Do you have any questions or ideas for how it might be better?

WRITING WORKSHOP

SHORT STORY

A short story is a short work of fiction. The writer's purpose is to entertain and to teach the reader something about life. Most short stories are about characters that writers invent, or make up, using their imagination. However, some stories are based on real people. Writers imagine what these people said and did. Characters in short stories usually have problems. As a character tries to solve a problem, he or she learns something about life.

A short story usually includes:

- one or more characters
- a setting—when and where the story happens
- a series of events, including a problem that one or more characters tries to solve
- a beginning, a middle, and an end

Write a short story about a character who learns something by solving a problem. Read the model that begins on the next page. Follow the steps below and on page 223.

 1 Prewrite Think about the stories you told in your group. What did each person learn by solving a problem? In this unit, think about what Bessie Coleman learned from flying. What did Aaron learn from taking care of Pidge?

Make a list of new ideas for a story. Discuss your ideas with a partner. Do you want to base your story on something that happened to someone you know? Do you want to write a story from your imagination?

Choose a story idea. Look at the outline on page 218. Make an outline to plan your story. For your main ideas (I, II, III), use number I for the beginning of your story, number II for the middle, and number III for the end. For details (A, B, etc.), include the setting, the character, the problem, other events, how the character solves the problem, and what he or she learns.

WRITING TIPS

Use dialogue to make your story more interesting to read.

- Remember to put dialogue in quotation marks. Here is an example: "Be careful," Aaron said. "I just took the bandages off."
- Use different verbs, such as *shouted* and *asked*, in your dialogue.
- Write dialogue that sounds natural—the way people really talk.

Before you write your story, read this model.

Haley Coy

The Summer of Friends

Maureen hung up the phone with her friend Tina. ← **Beginning**
When school was finished, Tina would be moving to New
York. "It's going to be a long, lonely summer," Maureen
thought sadly.

← **Problem: Maureen's friend moves away.**

A few days after Tina moved, Maureen saw something
in her backyard. Hiding near the fence was a gray kitten
with white paws. Maureen saw a tag around the kitten's
neck. It read: "My name is Socks. Please return me to the
Larsons."

Mrs. Larson lived on Maureen's street. She never spoke
to anyone. "Mrs. Larson's not very friendly," Maureen
thought. But she picked up the kitten and brought him to
Mrs. Larson's home anyway.

← **Middle**

"Thanks for finding Socks!" said Mrs. Larson with a
big smile. "Come in, Maureen. Have some cookies. I just
made them for my grandchildren. They're coming
tomorrow for the summer. You should come and meet
Gina. She's just about your age."

"Thanks, Mrs. Larson," Maureen said, taking a cookie.
"I'd love to meet Gina." Later, as she walked home,

Maureen thought, "I was wrong about Mrs. Larson. She's really nice."

The next day Maureen met Gina. They went swimming together and rode their bikes in the park. They became best friends.

Maureen had lost one friend, but she gained two— Mrs. Larson and Gina.

← End

← Solution: Maureen makes new friends.

2 **Draft** Use the model and your outline to help you write your story.

3 **Edit** Work with a partner. Trade papers and read each other's stories. Use the Editing Checklist below to evaluate your work.

EDITING CHECKLIST

Does your story . . .

▶ include a beginning, middle, and end?

▶ include dialogue in quotation marks?

▶ have correct spelling and punctuation?

4 **Revise** Rewrite parts of your story. Add details to make it more interesting. Correct mistakes if you need to.

5 **Publish** Share your work with your teacher and your classmates.

PROJECTS

Work in pairs or small groups. Choose one of these projects.

1 Make a timeline of "Great Events in the History of Flight." Include Bessie Coleman and other famous pilots and astronauts. Find or draw pictures for your timeline, and share it with the class.

2 Use the library or the Internet to research different ways to make an airplane out of paper, oak tag, or cardboard. Choose one way and make a paper plane. Write the steps for how you made your plane. Share your work with the class.

3 Bessie Coleman felt free when she flew her airplane. What makes you feel free? Make a collage of things that make you feel free. A collage is a kind of art you make by cutting and pasting pictures, photos, and other materials together. Share your collage with the class.

4 Cher Ami was a carrier pigeon who saved many American soldiers in World War I. Make a poster about another special animal. Use the library or the Internet to find information about your animal. Here are some interesting topic ideas:
- Belka and Strelka (two dogs who traveled into space)
- Koko (gorilla who learned American Sign Language)
- Fungie (wild dolphin who likes people)

5 The famous Greek myth of Daedalus and Icarus is about flight and freedom. Find this story in the library or on the Internet. Read the story. Then draw a comic strip that retells the story. Share your comic strip with the class.

6 Create a TV show in which you and a partner each review one movie. Tell the class what you liked and didn't like about the movies. Recommend that the class see—or not see—the movies.

To find out more about the theme of this unit, choose from these reading suggestions.

Amelia and Eleanor Go for a Ride, **Pam Muñoz Ryan** This book tells about an event that really happened. On April 20, 1933, First Lady Eleanor Roosevelt and pilot Amelia Earhart left a formal dinner party at the White House to enjoy a plane ride around Washington, D.C. Then, before they returned to the White House, they took the same tour by car.

Talkin' about Bessie: The Story of Aviator Elizabeth Coleman, **Nikki Grimes** The author imagines the story of Bessie Coleman's life as told by people who knew her, including her parents, her sisters and brothers, a teacher, a newspaper publisher, a flight instructor, and two reporters. As each person gives a new point of view about Bessie, the reader learns about what a special person she was.

This Big Sky, **Pat Mora** This collection of fourteen poems celebrates the American Southwest. Pat Mora's poetry is spare; the words are simple. Yet the images her poetry evokes range from playful to deeply mysterious. The poems in this book are sure to delight readers of varying ages and reading abilities.

Apollo 13, **Dina Anastasio** It is April of 1970, and Jim Lovell, Fred Haise, and Jack Swigert are flying the *Apollo 13* spaceship to the moon. Suddenly something goes wrong. They hear a loud noise. Then the ship starts to lose oxygen and power. The astronauts cannot fly the ship without power, and they cannot live without air. Will they get home to Earth? Read this book to find out.

Bird, **David Burnie** Among the many topics you will learn about in this book are how birds' bodies are designed for flight, why their wings are different shapes and sizes, and how many feathers birds have and what each one does. The book contains hundreds of colorful photos and illustrations about the history, behavior, and life cycle of birds.

Phonics Handbook

CONSONANT SOUNDS AND THEIR SPELLINGS

Some letters are called consonants. The **con** part of the word **consonant** means "with." The **sonant** part means "sound." Consonants are letters that stand for speech sounds. Consonant speech sounds go with vowel sounds and other consonant sounds when we speak.

A consonant spelling goes with vowel spellings and other consonant spellings when we write.

Pages 227–235 of this handbook show you twenty-five consonant sounds and how they are spelled. A symbol for each sound is shown in slashes like this //.

Spellings of each consonant sound are shown in color in the samples.

Key words show you words that have this consonant sound. The key words show examples of the sound's spelling at the beginning, middle, or end of the words.

This is the sound symbol.

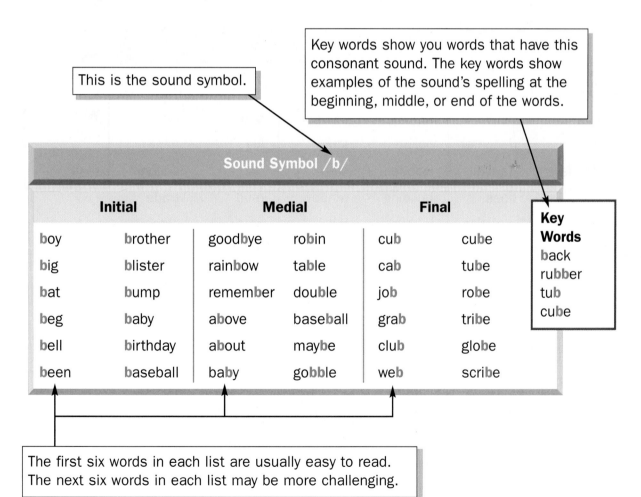

Sound Symbol /b/

Initial		Medial		Final	
boy	brother	goodbye	robin	cub	cube
big	blister	rainbow	table	cab	tube
bat	bump	remember	double	job	robe
beg	baby	above	baseball	grab	tribe
bell	birthday	about	maybe	club	globe
been	baseball	baby	gobble	web	scribe

Key Words
back
rubber
tub
cube

The first six words in each list are usually easy to read.
The next six words in each list may be more challenging.

CONSONANT SOUNDS AND THEIR SPELLINGS

Sound Symbol /p/

Initial		Medial		Final	
pad	plenty	copy	shopping	tip	hiccup
pet	pancake	sample	repeat	stop	gallop
pick	pickle	hoping	report	clap	hope
pill	pineapple	kept	pineapple	jump	ape
pants	pumpkin	slept	pumpkin	keep	ripe
pretty		open	supper	sleep	shape

Key Words
pack
happy
cape

Sound Symbol /d/

Initial		Medial		Final	
dog	different	reading	addition	bad	said
dig	daughter	children	study	kid	hand
do, dew	daylight	wooden	idea	bed	second
down	does	building	window	mud	trade
deep	direction	middle	today	hold	side
drop	December	medal	riding	third	include

Key Words
day
student
read

Sound Symbol /t/

Initial		Medial		Final	
to, too, two	television	city	attack	but, butt	right, write
tan	tomorrow	interview	kitten	aunt, ant	night
tell	traffic	interesting	butter	lost	cute
told	terrible	beautiful	matter	dirt	brought
take	tornado	adjective	pretty	boot	fought
time	Tuesday	entertain	bitter	melt	Internet

Key Words
tie
batter
ant

Sound Symbol /g/

Initial		Medial		Final	
gas	gold	ago	bigger	big	egg
get	good	begin	giggle	bag	flag
girl	group	began	logging	rug	smog
give	grow	together	logo	rag	smug
gone	ground	figure	regret	beg	catalog
game	government	forgotten	struggle	frog	travelogue

Key Words
go
forget
leg

Sound Symbol /k/

Initial		Medial		Final	
cut	kitten	became	recall	black	disk
cap	cola	because	unclear	kick	thank
come	comment	raincoat	ecology	like	music
kept	cream	backward	echo	walk	fantastic
kite	camel	picnic	except	talk	break
color	chorus		excite	sink	mistake

Key Words
cat
key
chorus
become
ticket
lake
back
arc

Sound Symbol /v/

Initial		Medial		Final	
very	valley	never	shove	have	drive
visit	view	ever	shiver	cave	drove
violin	value	over	invest	give	move
voice	vital	even	review	live	twelve
vowel	villain	eleven	prove	five	believe
visa	victory	cover	move	of	relieve

Key Words
van
river
love

CONSONANT SOUNDS AND THEIR SPELLINGS

Sound Symbol /f/

Initial		Medial		Final		Key Words
for	funny	after	beautiful	if	life	fan
find	found	before	cupful	off	half	photo
first	face	often	snowflake	wolf	laugh	offer
fire	family	careful	afraid	half	graph	golf
feet	friends	different	telephone	myself	enough	tough
fish	February	outfit	coughing	cliff	rough	

Sound Symbol /ð/

Initial		Medial		Final	Key Words
this	their	father	northern	smooth	the
that	they	mother	leather	breathe	whether
there	these	brother	farther	writhe	weather
them	then	other	together	scythe	bathe
those	than	either	gather	tithe	
though		feather	soothing		

Sound Symbol /θ/

Initial		Medial		Final		Key Words
throw	thousand	anything	author	with	cloth	three
threw	thunder	nothing	birthday	tooth	math	something
thank	thirty	athlete	mathematics	teeth	south	bath
think	thirteen	bathrobe	without	fifth	north	
thing	thick	bathtub	earthquake	earth	both	
thumb	Thursday	toothbrush	northeast	truth	worth	

230

Sound Symbol /z/

Initial		Medial		Final		Key Words
zip	zap	lazy	citizen	jazz	as	zoo
zero	zeal	puzzle	organized	quiz	is	easy
zoom	zest	dozen	magazine	freeze	flies	runs
zebra	zinc	frozen	rising	prize	was	buzz
zipper	zoology	breezy	choosing	size	says	rise
zone		music		please	wise	

Sound Symbol /s/

Initial		Medial		Final		Key Words
sat	science	also	pencil	books	address	sun
sell, cell	cent	person	decide	units	across	city
soon	cereal	answer	percent	products	ice	best
said	citizen	inside	dancing	marks	advice	less
so, sew	certain	lesson	bicycle	plus	place	fence
sea, see	circus	herself		less	force	

Sound Symbol /ʒ/

	Medial		Final	Key Words
	treasure	division	beige	vision
	pleasure	revision	rouge	beige
	leisure			
	casual			
	Caucasian			
	azure			

231

CONSONANT SOUNDS AND THEIR SPELLINGS

Sound Symbol /ʃ/

Initial		Medial		Final	
she	show	washing	machine	wish	leash
ship	shower	bushes	station	fish	finish
short	shell	brushed	vacation	rush	punish
shape	shame	cushion	addition	wash	publish
shoes	chef	fraction	subtraction	ash	establish
shine	chic	description	magician	push	abolish

Key Words
shop
fishing
nation
musician
dish

Sound Symbol /h/

Initial				Medial	
he	here	house	hospital	ahead	rehearse
his	have	horse	heard	behind	inherit
her	has	high	happened	overhead	inhuman
how	half	hand	hundred	behave	unheard
home	hill	head	hair	household	withhold
happy	help	hard	hole	uphill	downhill

Key Words
hot
unhappy

Sound Symbol /tʃ/

Initial		Medial		Final	
chip	chapter	lunchroom	pitcher	pinch	itch
chin	champion	branches	catcher	rich	ditch
chop	chew	unchanged	structure	bunch	pitch
cheek	chalk	inches	century	coach	watch
cheap	cheer	teacher	lecture	peach	fetch
child	children		actually	reach	March

Key Words
check
lunches
ketchup
picture
such
match

Sound Symbol /dʒ/

Initial		Medial		Final	
jam	gym, Jim	magic	algebra	cage	huge
jar	genes, jeans	tragic	biology	wage	large
jacket	genius	region	ecology	range	fudge
general	June	register		change	badge
geography	July	majority		strange	hinge
generous	January	legislate		bridge	singe

Key Words
giant
joy
biology
legend
judge

Sound Symbol /m/

Initial		Medial		Final	
my	much	family	remove	am	system
many	miles	example	important	him, hymn	come
more	music	number	immediately	harm	name
man	morning	became	summer	farm	some
must	May	remain	government	swim	limb
means	Monday	sometimes	camera	time	comb

Key Words
mother
animal
seem
home
lamb

Sound Symbol /n/

Initial		Medial		Final	
no, know	number	under	inches	in	children
net	notice	second	front	on	done
new, knew	note	once	scientist	one	person
near	nothing	wonder	manner	run	shown, shone
never	next	stand	inner	down	machine
not, knot	noun	ground		upon	plane, plain

Key Words
nest
know
mind
cannot
fun
cone

CONSONANT SOUNDS AND THEIR SPELLINGS

Sound Symbol /ŋ/

	Medial		Final	
	fangs	language	song	strong
	tongs	tangles	wrong	floating
	jungle	single	long	going
	hanger	youngster	lung	running
	singer	kingdom	spring	watering
	lengthen	longed	thing	sitting

Key Words
stronger
sing

Sound Symbol /l/

Initial		Medial		Final	
lip	large	alive	reply	real, reel	small
look	learn	only	world	seal	tell
like	light	belong	palace	wheel	vowel
live	land	family	follow	girl	hole
list	lunch	really	wealthy	heal, heel	single
long	little	smaller	schoolroom	people	regular

Key Words
last
slowly
pull
bottle
until

Sound Symbol /r/

Initial		Medial		Final	
red	rudder	girls	overcome	our	other
ran	review	worked	largest	are	after
read, reed	ready	three	different	year	before
room	religion	earth	triangle	here, hear	there, their
road	right, write	learn	Thursday	for, four	near
reef	wrong	hungry	Friday	water	square

Key Words
run
very
far
care

Sound Symbol /w/

Initial		Medial	
we	were	forward	awake
will	word	backward	rework
was	world	upward	between
water	want	halfway	northwest
way, weigh	woman	sandwich	catwalk
walk	Wednesday	unwilling	highway

Key Words
win
away

Sound Symbol /hw/

Initial		Medial	
when	wheel	everywhere	awhile
where	whip	meanwhile	buckwheat
which	while	cartwheel	overwhelm
why	whale	somewhat	bobwhite
whether	whine	somewhere	
wheat	whistle	anywhere	

Key Words
white
nowhere

Sound Symbol /y/

Initial		Medial	
yes	you	papaya	lawyer
year	your	backyard	vineyard
yen	young	barnyard	beyond
yellow	yak	courtyard	
yet	yoga	canyon	
yard	yesterday	unyielding	

Key Words
you
yoyo

VOWEL SOUNDS AND THEIR SPELLINGS

Vowel sounds are speech sounds. A vowel sound in a word usually lasts longer than a consonant sound.

Vowels are also letters. Vowel letters are **a, e, i, o, u,** and sometimes **y.** Vowel letters sometimes go together in pairs such as **ai, ea, oi,** and **ay.**

This handbook shows you sixteen speech sounds that are spelled with one or two vowel letters. The word **bat** is an example of a word that has one vowel letter and vowel sound. The word **banana** is an example of a word with three vowel letters and vowel sounds. The word **antidisestablishmentarianism** has eleven vowel letters and sounds. It is one of the longest words in English.

Key words show you examples of words with the vowel sound. The key words show you ways that the vowel sound is spelled. The vowel sound is in color.

This is the symbol that stands for the vowel sound.

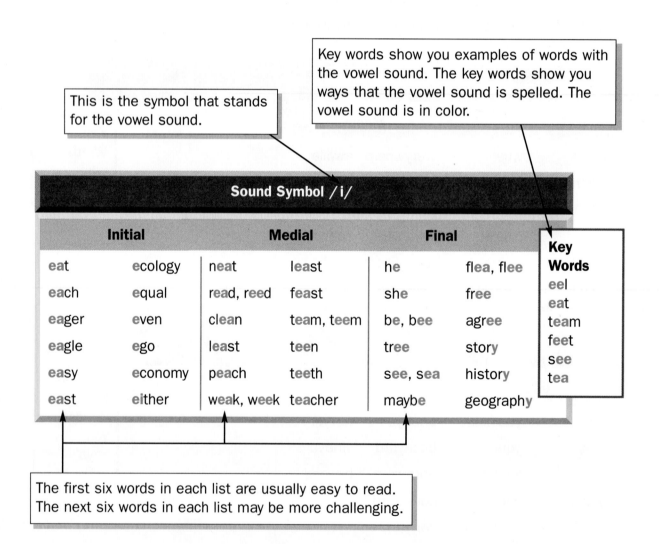

Sound Symbol /i/

Initial		Medial		Final		Key Words
eat	ecology	neat	least	he	flea, flee	eel
each	equal	read, reed	feast	she	free	eat
eager	even	clean	team, teem	be, bee	agree	team
eagle	ego	least	teen	tree	story	feet
easy	economy	peach	teeth	see, sea	history	see
east	either	weak, week	teacher	maybe	geography	tea

The first six words in each list are usually easy to read. The next six words in each list may be more challenging.

Sound Symbol /ɪ/

Initial		Medial			
in	insect	did	giving		
if	igloo	with	whip		
is	instant	his	silver		
inch	itself	this	hidden		
into	inform	little	finger		
illness	interrupt	city	gym		

Key Words
it
win
swinging

Sound Symbol /eɪ/

Initial		Medial		Final	
ate, eight	aged	gave	baseball	hey	weigh
apron	acre	state	playoff	they	neigh
agent	ail, ale	main, mane	daylight	obey	sleigh
able	ache	quake	volcano	stay	gangway
aim	eighteen	straight, strait	neighbor	today	birthday
aide	April	equation	rain, reign	bluejay	Saturday

Key Words
rain
gate
they
say

Sound Symbol /ɛ/

Initial		Medial		
egg	explain	ten	next	bread
ever	enjoy	send	spelling	head
extra	engine	when	helpful	dead
edge	enter	then	melon	said
elephant	exit	get	themselves	says
		let	together	

Key Words
end
bed

VOWEL SOUNDS AND THEIR SPELLINGS

Sound Symbol /æ/

Initial		Medial	
at	addition	that	than
as	adjective	have	happen
act	answer	can	began
add	actor	fact	planted
ask	animal	black	vacuum
ant	axle	hand	

Key Words
and
had

Sound Symbol /ɑ/

Initial		Medial	
on	observation	not, knot	clock
ox	obvious	box	bottom
olive	oddity	hot	product
opera	operation	stop	copy
object	opportunity	job	comrade
octopus	October	crop	concentration

Key Words
odd
top

Sound Symbol /ɔ/

Initial		Medial	
all	awning	salt	walk
also	author	false	chalk
although	auto	call	crawl
always	audio	ball, bawl	caution
already	auditorium	mall, maul	because
altogether	August	stall	bought

Key Words
awesome
caught
mall
talk
cough

Sound Symbol /oʊ/

Initial		Medial		Final	
oh, owe	only	poem	coat	go	echo
open	own	program	road	hello	volcano
over	oats	total	loaded	also	show
ocean	oak	broken	floating	zero	row
obey	oath	home	known	radio	tomorrow
okay, OK		alone	bowling	piano	yellow

Key Words
old
pole
boat
no
snow

Sound Symbol /ʊ/

	Medial	
	look	push
	took	pull
	book	pulley
	good	cookie
	wood	understood
	hoof	neighborhood

Key Words
book
foot
put

Sound Symbol /u/

Initial	Medial		Final	
ooze	cool	troop, troupe	do, dew, due	grew
oodles	food	tooth	to, too, two	zoo
oops	balloon	truce	blue	who
	boot	loose	flew, flu, flue	issue
	smooth	soon	crew	tissue
	group	Tuesday	new, knew	you, yew

Key Words
ooze
pool
spruce
soup
stew
true

VOWEL SOUNDS AND THEIR SPELLINGS

Sound Symbol /aɪ/

Initial		Medial		Final	
I, eye	iron	time	life	high, hi	fly
ice	icon	like	while	sigh	sty
icy	iota	find	sight, site, cite	reply	tie
aisle, isle	ion	light	title	by, buy	beautify
item	ivy	right	flying	my	magnify
iris	ivory	night	trying	lie, lye	purify

Key Words
idea
pilot
smile
cry
pie

Sound Symbol /aʊ/

Initial		Medial		Final	
ouch	outcry	about	towel	how	vow
our	outlook	down	mountain	cow	snowplow
outdoors	ounce	sound	vowel	somehow	
ourselves	outfield	around	proud	bow	
outline	owl	ground	loud	eyebrow	
outside	oust	howl	mouth	sow	

Key Words
out
owl
pound
hound
allow

Sound Symbol /ɔɪ/

Initial	Medial		Final	
oyster	point	appointment	boy	employ
oink	join	enjoyment	joy	cowboy
oily	soil	soybean	coy	alloy
oilcloth	voice	voyage	destroy	corduroy
ointment	coin	loyal	annoy	decoy
oilwell	royal	employee	enjoy	Troy

Key Words
oil
noise
royal
toy

Sound Symbol /ʌ/

Initial		Medial		Key Words
us	upset	but	submarine	up
under	unseen	much	number	cut
ugly	unpack	jump	son, sun	something
uncle	unnecessary	summer	someone	trouble
upper	umpire	funny	double	front
utter	understand	front	frontier	

Sound Symbol /ɚ/

Initial		Medial		Final		Key Words
earn, urn	earth	govern	squirrel	fir	sure	earth
early	urban	liberty	turn	stir	future	bird
earnings	urgent	western	burned	her	creature	hurry
earthworm	earnest	butterfly	church	player	terror	humor
urge	earthquake	circus	hurdle	answer	rumor, roomer	teacher
irk		dirt	worry	November		feature

Sound Symbol /ə/

Initial		Medial		Final		Key Words
ago	opinion	level	second	idea	iguana	about
again	occur	different	focus	antenna	lava	banana
away	until	animal	family	comma	fava	
aside	upon	together	fasten	bandanna	retina	
above	unless	often	guacamole	guava	sauna	
official	upholstery	children		mantilla	saga	

Grammar, Usage, and Mechanics Handbook

THE PARTS OF SPEECH

In English, there are eight **parts of speech**: nouns, pronouns, adjectives, verbs, adverbs, prepositions, conjunctions, and interjections.

NOUNS

Nouns name people, places, or things. There are two kinds of nouns: **common nouns** and **proper nouns**.

A **common noun** is a general person, place, or thing.

person	thing	place

The **student** brings a **notebook** to **class**.

A **proper noun** is a specific person, place, or thing. Proper nouns start with a capital letter.

person	place	thing

Margaret goes to **California** every **June**.

A noun that is made up of two words is called a **compound noun**. A compound noun can be one word or two words. Some compound nouns have hyphens.

One word: **newspaper**, **bathroom**
Two words: **vice president**, **pet shop**
Hyphens: **sister-in-law**, **grown-up**

Articles identify nouns. *A, an,* and *the* are articles.

A and *an* are called **indefinite articles**. Use the article *a* or *an* to talk about one general person, place, or thing.

Use *an* before a word that begins with a vowel sound.

I have **an** idea.

Use *a* before a word that begins with a consonant sound.

> May I borrow **a** pen?

The is called a **definite article**. Use *the* to talk about one or more specific people, places, or things.

> Please bring me **the** box from your room.
> **The** books are in my backpack.

PRONOUNS

Pronouns are words that take the place of nouns or proper nouns. In this example, the pronoun *she* replaces, or refers to, the proper noun *Anita.*

proper noun   pronoun
Anita is not home. **She** is babysitting.

Pronouns can be subjects or objects. They can be singular or plural.

	Subject Pronouns	**Object Pronouns**
Singular	I, you, he, she, it	me, you, him, her, it
Plural	we, you, they	us, you, them

A **subject pronoun** replaces a noun or proper noun that is the subject of a sentence. A **subject** is who or what a sentence is about. In these sentences, *He* replaces *Dan.*

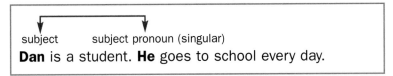

subject   subject pronoun (singular)
Dan is a student. **He** goes to school every day.

In these sentences, *We* replaces *Jaime* and *I.*

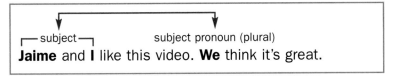

subject   subject pronoun (plural)
Jaime and **I** like this video. **We** think it's great.

An **object pronoun** replaces a noun or proper noun that is the object of a verb. A verb tells the action in a sentence. An **object** receives the action of a verb.

In these sentences, the verb is *gave. Him* replaces *Ed,* which is the object of the verb.

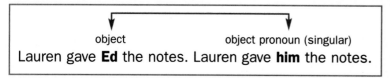

object   object pronoun (singular)

Lauren gave **Ed** the notes. Lauren gave **him** the notes.

An object pronoun can also replace a noun or proper noun that is the **object of a preposition**. Prepositions are words like *for, to,* or *with.* In these sentences, the preposition is *with. Them* replaces *José and Yolanda,* which is the object of the preposition.

object of a preposition   object pronoun (plural)

I went to the mall with **José and Yolanda**. I went to the mall with **them**.

Pronouns can also be possessive. A **possessive pronoun** replaces a noun or proper noun. It shows who owns something.

	Possessive Pronouns
Singular	mine, yours, hers, his
Plural	ours, yours, theirs

In these sentences, *hers* replaces the words *Alicia's coat.* It shows that Alicia owns the coat.

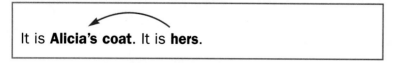

It is **Alicia's coat**. It is **hers**.

ADJECTIVES

Adjectives describe nouns. An adjective usually comes before the noun it describes.

tall grass   **big** truck   **two** kittens

An adjective can come *after* the noun it describes. This happens in these kinds of sentences.

The book bag is **heavy**. The books are **old**.

Do not add -s to adjectives that describe plural nouns.

the **red** houses   the **funny** jokes   the **smart** teachers

VERBS

Verbs express an action or a state of being.

subject verb   subject verb   Jack **walks** to school. The school **is** near his house.

An **action verb** tells what someone or something does or did. You cannot always see the action of an action verb.

Verbs That Tell Actions You Can See	Verbs That Tell Actions You Cannot See
dance swim	know sense
play talk	remember name
sit write	think understand

A **linking verb** shows no action. It links the subject with another word that describes the subject.

Linking Verbs		
look	is	appear
smell	are	seem
sound	am	become
taste	were	
feel		

In this sentence, the adjective *tired* tells something about the subject, *dog*. *Seems* is the linking verb.

Our dog **seems** tired.

In this sentence, the noun *friend* tells something about the subject, *brother*. *Is* is the linking verb.

Your brother **is** my friend.

A **helping verb** comes before the main verb. It adds to the main verb's meaning. Helping verbs can be forms of the verb *be, do,* or *have.*

	Helping Verbs
Forms of the verb *be*	am, was, is, were, are
Forms of the verb *do*	do, did, does
Forms of the verb *have*	have, had, has
Other helping verbs	can, must, could, have (to), should, may, will, would

In this sentence, *am* is the helping verb; *walking* is the action verb.

helping   action
  verb   verb
I **am walking** to my English class.

In this sentence, *has* is the helping verb; *completed* is the action verb.

helping   action
  verb   verb
He **has completed** his report.

In questions, the subject comes between a helping verb and a main verb.

> subject
> **Did** Liang **give** you the CD?

ADVERBS

Adverbs describe the action of verbs. They tell *how* an action happens. Adverbs answer the question *Where? When? How?* or *How much?* or *How often?*

Many adverbs end in *-ly.*

> easily   slowly   carefully

Some adverbs do not end in *-ly.*

> seldom   fast   very

In this sentence, the adverb *everywhere* modifies the verb *looked.* It answers the question *Where?*

> verb   adverb
> Nicole looked **everywhere** for her ring.

In this sentence, the adverb *quickly* modifies the verb *walked.* It answers the question *How?*

> verb   adverb
> They walked home **quickly**.

Adverbs also modify adjectives. They answer the question *How much?* or *How little?*

In this sentence, the adjective *dangerous* modifies the noun *road.* The adverb *very* modifies the adjective *dangerous.*

> adverb   adjective   noun
> This is a **very** dangerous road.

Adverbs can also modify other adverbs. In this sentence, the adverb *fast* modifies the verb *runs.* The adverb *quite* modifies the adverb *fast.*

> verb adverb adverb
> Joe runs **quite** fast.

PREPOSITIONS

Prepositions can show time, place, and direction.

Time	Place	Direction
after	above	across
before	below	down
during	in	into
since	near	to
until	under	up

In this sentence, the preposition *above* shows where the bird flew. It shows place.

> preposition
> A bird flew **above** my head.

In this sentence, the preposition *across* shows direction.

> preposition
> The children walked **across** the street.

A **prepositional phrase** starts with a preposition and ends with a noun or pronoun.

In this sentence, the preposition is *near* and the noun is *school.*

```
                    ┌─ prepositional phrase ─┐
The library is near the new school.
```

CONJUNCTIONS

A **conjunction** joins words, groups of words, and whole sentences.

Conjunctions	
and	nor
but	yet
or	so
for	

In this sentence, the conjunction *and* joins two proper nouns: *Allison* and *Teresa.*

```
 noun         noun
Allison and Teresa are in school.
```

In this sentence, the conjunction *or* joins two prepositional phrases: *to the movies* and *to the mall.*

```
                 prepositional    prepositional
                  ┌─ phrase ─┐    ┌─ phrase ─┐
They want to go to the movies or to the mall.
```

In this sentence, the conjunction *and* joins two independent clauses: *Alana baked the cookies,* and *Eric made the lemonade.*

```
┌── independent clause ──┐  ┌── independent clause ──┐
Alana baked the cookies, and Eric made the lemonade.
```

INTERJECTIONS

Interjections are words or phrases that express emotion.

Interjections that express strong emotion are followed by an exclamation point.

> **Wow!** Did you see that catch?
> **Hey!** Watch out for the ball!

Interjections that express mild emotion are followed by a comma.

> **Gee,** I'm sorry that your team lost.
> **Oh,** it's OK. We'll do better next time.

CLAUSES

Clauses are groups of words with a subject and a verb. Some clauses form complete sentences; they tell a complete thought. Others do not.

This clause is a complete sentence. Clauses that form complete sentences are called **independent clauses**.

>   subject   verb
> The dog's **tail wagged**.

This clause is not a complete sentence. Clauses that don't form complete sentences are called **dependent clauses**.

>   subject verb
> when the **boy pet** him

Independent clauses can be combined with dependent clauses to form a sentence.

In this sentence, *The dog's tail wagged* is an independent clause. *When the boy pet him* is a dependent clause.

```
┌─ independent clause ─┐ ┌─ dependent clause ─┐
The dog's tail wagged when the boy pet him.
```

SENTENCES

Sentences have a subject and a verb, and tell a complete thought. A sentence always begins with a capital letter. It always ends with a period, question mark, or exclamation point.

```
                subject   action verb
           The cheetah runs very fast.

   helping verb   subject   action verb
           Do you play soccer?

        subject   linking verb
            I am so late!
```

SIMPLE SENTENCES AND COMPOUND SENTENCES

Some sentences are called simple sentences. Others are called compound sentences. A **simple sentence** has one independent clause. Here is an example.

```
┌─ independent clause ─────────────┐
The dog barked at the mail carrier.
```

Compound sentences are made up of two or more simple sentences, or independent clauses. They are joined together by a **conjunction** such as *and* or *but*.

```
┌─── independent clause ───┐ ┌─ independent clause ─┐
The band has a lead singer, but they need a drummer.
```

SENTENCE TYPES

Sentences have different purposes. There are four types of sentences: declarative, interrogative, imperative, and exclamatory.

Declarative sentences are statements. They end with a period.

> We are going to the beach on Saturday**.**

Interrogative sentences are questions. They end with a question mark.

> Will you come with us**?**

Imperative sentences are commands. They usually end with a period. If the command is strong, the sentence may end with an exclamation point.

> Put on your life jacket. Now jump into the water**!**

Exclamatory sentences express strong feeling. They end with an exclamation point.

> I swam all the way from the boat to the shore**!**

MECHANICS

END MARKS

End marks come at the end of sentences. There are three kinds of end marks: periods, question marks, and exclamation points.

Use a **period** to end a statement (declarative sentence).

> The spacecraft *Magellan* took pictures of Jupiter**.**

Use a **period** to end a command or request (imperative sentence) that isn't strong enough to need an exclamation point.

> Please change the channel**.**

Use a **question mark** to end a sentence that asks a question (interrogative sentence).

> Where does Mrs. Contreras live**?**

Use an **exclamation point** to end a sentence that expresses strong feeling (exclamatory sentence).

> That was a great party**!**
> Look at that huge house**!**

Use an **exclamation point** to end an imperative sentence that gives a strong command.

> Don't get too close to the pool**!**

Periods are also used after initials and many abbreviations.

Use a **period** after a person's initial or abbreviated title.

Ms. Susan Vargas	Mrs. Fiske	J. D. Salinger
Gov. Lise Crawford	Mr. Vargas	Dr. Sapirstein

Use a **period** after the abbreviation of streets, roads, and so on.

Avenue ⟶ Ave.	Road ⟶ Rd.
Boulevard ⟶ Blvd.	Street ⟶ St.
Highway ⟶ Hwy.	

Use a **period** after the abbreviation of many units of measurement. Abbreviations for metric units do *not* use periods.

inch ⟶ in.	centimeter ⟶ cm
foot ⟶ ft.	meter ⟶ m
pound ⟶ lb.	kilogram ⟶ kg
gallon ⟶ gal.	liter ⟶ l

COMMAS

Commas separate, or set off, parts of a sentence or phrase.

Use a comma to separate two independent clauses linked by a conjunction. In this sentence, the comma goes before the conjunction *but.*

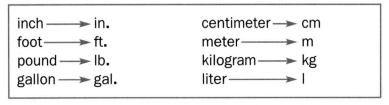
independent clause · independent clause
We went to the museum, **but** it was closed.

Use commas to separate the parts in a series. A series is a group of three or more words, phrases, or very brief clauses.

	Commas in Series
To separate words	Lucio's bike is red, white, and silver.
To separate phrases	Today, he rode over the lawn, down the sidewalk, and up the hill.
To separate clauses	Lucio washed the bike, his dad washed the car, and his mom washed the dog.

Use a comma to set off an introductory word, phrase, or clause.

	Commas with Introductory Words
To set off a word	Yes, Stacy likes to go swimming. Alma, do you like to swim?
To set off a phrase	In a month, she may join the swim team again.
To set off a clause	If she joins the swim team, I'll miss her at softball practice.

Use commas to set off an interrupting word, phrase, or clause.

	Commas with Interrupting Words
To set off a word	We left, finally, to get some fresh air.
To set off a phrase	Carol's dog, a brown pug, shakes when he gets scared.
To set off a clause	The assignment, I'm sorry to say, was too hard for me.

Use a comma to set off a speaker's quoted words in a sentence.

> Jeanne asked, "Where is that book I just had?"
> "I just saw it," said Billy, "on the kitchen counter."

In a **direct address**, one speaker talks directly to another. Use commas to set off the name of the person being addressed.

> Thank you, Dee, for helping to put away the dishes.
> Sophia, why are you late again?

Use a comma between the day and the year.

> My cousin was born on September 9, 2001.

If the date appears in the middle of a sentence, use a comma before *and* after the year.

> Daria's mother was born on June 8, 1965, in New Jersey.

Use a comma between a city and a state and between a city and a nation.

> My father grew up in Bakersfield, California.
> We are traveling to Acapulco, Mexico.

If the names appear in the middle of a sentence, use a comma before *and* after the state or nation.

> My friend Carl went to Bombay, India, last year.

Use a comma after the greeting in a friendly letter. Use a comma after the closing in both a friendly letter and formal letter. Do this in e-mail letters, too.

> Dear Margaret,   Sincerely,   Yours truly,

SEMICOLONS AND COLONS

Semicolons can connect two independent clauses. Use them when the clauses are closely related in meaning or structure.

> The team won again; it was their ninth victory.
> Ana usually studies right after school; Rita prefers to study in the evening.

Colons introduce a list of items or important information.

Use a colon after an independent clause to introduce a list of items. (The clause often has the words *as follows, the following, these, those,* or *this*.)

> The following animals live in Costa Rica: monkeys, lemurs, toucans, and jaguars.

Use a colon to introduce important information. If the information is in an independent clause, use a capital letter to begin the first word after the colon.

> There is one main rule: Do not talk to anyone during the test.
> You must remember this: Stay away from the train tracks!

Use a colon to separate hours and minutes when writing the time.

> 1:30   7:45   11:08

QUOTATION MARKS

Quotation marks set off direct quotations, dialogue, and some titles. A **direct quotation** is the exact words that somebody said, wrote, or thought.

Commas and periods *always* go inside quotation marks. If a question mark or exclamation point is part of the quotation, it is also placed *inside* the quotation marks.

> "Can you please get ready**?**" Mom asked.
> My sister shouted, "Look out for that bee**!**"

If a question mark or exclamation point is *not* part of the quotation, it goes *outside* the quotation marks. In these cases there is no punctuation before the end quotation marks.

> Did you say, "I can't do this"**?**

Conversation between two or more people is called **dialogue**. Use quotation marks to set off dialogue words.

> "What a great ride!" Pam said. "Let's go on it again."
> José shook his head and said, "No way. I'm feeling sick."

Use quotation marks around the titles of short works of writing or other art forms. The following kinds of titles take quotation marks:

Chapters	"The Railroad in the West"
Short Stories	"The Perfect Cat"
Articles	"California in the 1920s"
Songs	"This Land Is Your Land"
Single TV episodes	"Charlie's New Idea"
Short poems	"The Bat"

Titles of all other written work and artwork are underlined. These include books, magazines, newspapers, plays, movies, TV series, and paintings.

APOSTROPHES

Apostrophes can be used with singular and plural nouns to show ownership or possession. To form the possessive, follow these rules:

For singular nouns: Add an apostrophe and an s.

Maria**'s** eyes   hamster**'s** cage   the sun**'s** warmth

For singular nouns that end in s: Add an apostrophe and an s to these nouns, too.

her boss**'s** office   Carlos**'s** piano   the grass**'s** length

For plural nouns that do not end in s: Add an apostrophe and an s.

women**'s** clothes   men**'s** shoes   children**'s** books

For plural nouns that end in s: Add an apostrophe.

teachers' lounge   dogs' leashes   kids' playground

Apostrophes are also used in **contractions**. A contraction is a shortened form of two words that have been combined. The apostrophe shows where a letter or letters have been taken away.

I will **I'll** be home in one hour.   do not We **don't** have any soup.

CAPITALIZATION
There are five main reasons to use capital letters:
1. to begin a sentence and in a direct quotation
2. to write the word *I*
3. to write the name of a specific person, place, or thing
4. to write a person's title
5. to write the title of a work (artwork, written work)

Use a capital letter to begin the first word in a sentence.

> **C**ows eat grass. **T**hey also eat hay.

Use a capital letter for the first word of a direct quotation. Use the capital letter even if the quotation is in the middle of a sentence.

> Sophie said, "**W**e need more sand for the sand castle."

Use a capital letter for the word *I*.

> How will **I** ever learn all these things? **I** guess **I** will learn them little by little.

Use a capital letter for the name of a specific person, place, or thing. Capitalize the important words in names.

> **R**obert **E. L**ee   **M**exico   **T**uesday   **T**ropic of **C**ancer

Capital Letters in Place Names	
Streets	Interstate 95, Center Street, Atwood Avenue
City Sections	Greenwich Village, Shaker Heights, East Side
Cities and Towns	Rome, Chicago, Fresno
States	California, North Dakota, Maryland
Regions	Pacific Northwest, Great Plains, Eastern Europe
Nations	China, Dominican Republic, Italy
Continents	North America, Africa, Asia
Mountains	Mount Shasta, Andes Mountains, Rocky Mountains
Deserts	Mojave Desert, Sahara Desert, Gobi Desert
Islands	Fiji Islands, Capri, Virgin Islands
Rivers	Amazon River, Nile River, Mississippi River
Lakes	Lake Superior, Great Bear Lake, Lake Tahoe
Bays	San Francisco Bay, Hudson Bay, Galveston Bay
Seas	Mediterranean Sea, Sea of Japan
Oceans	Pacific Ocean, Atlantic Ocean, Indian Ocean

Capital Letters for Specific Things	
Historical Periods, Events	Renaissance, Battle of Bull Run
Historical Texts	Constitution, Bill of Rights
Days and Months	Monday, October
Holidays	Thanksgiving, Labor Day
Organizations, Schools	Greenpeace, Central High School
Government Bodies	Congress, State Department
Political Parties	Republican Party, Democratic Party
Ethnic Groups	Chinese, Latinos
Languages, Nationalities	Spanish, Canadian
Buildings	Empire State Building, City Hall
Monuments	Lincoln Memorial, Washington Monument
Religions	Hinduism, Christianity, Judaism, Islam

Use a capital letter for a person's title if the title comes before the name. In the second sentence below, a capital letter is not needed because the title does not come before a name.

> I heard **S**enator Clinton's speech about jobs.
> The **s**enator may come to our school.

Use a capital letter for the first and last word and all other important words in titles of books, newspapers, magazines, short stories, plays, movies, songs, paintings, and sculptures.

> Lucy wants to read **The Lord of the R**ings.
> The newspaper my father reads is the **New York Times**.
> Did you like the painting called **Work in the F**ields?
> This poem is called "**The Birch Tree**."

Reading Resources Handbook

DICTIONARY

You can find the **spelling, pronunciation, part of speech,** and **definitions** of words in the dictionary. Many words in English have more than one meaning. Some words, such as *court,* can be both a noun and a verb. The part of speech is usually abbreviated (*n* for *noun, v* for *verb, adj* for *adjective,* and *adv* for *adverb*). The part of speech comes after the word's pronunciation. Then the meanings, or definitions, are numbered. Sometimes **example sentences** are given in italics.

Here is a sample dictionary **entry** for the word *court.* You learned one meaning of *court* in Unit 3. This entry gives that definition and others:

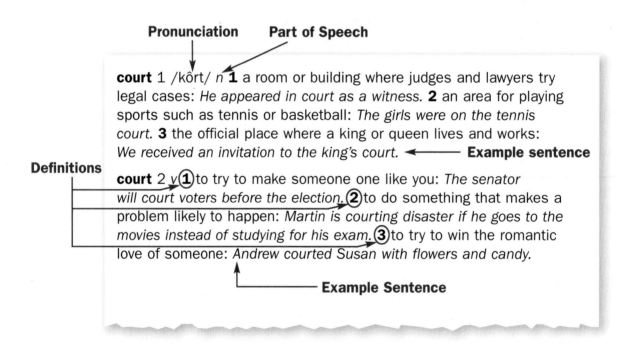

Pronunciation   **Part of Speech**

court 1 /kôrt/ *n* **1** a room or building where judges and lawyers try legal cases: *He appeared in court as a witness.* **2** an area for playing sports such as tennis or basketball: *The girls were on the tennis court.* **3** the official place where a king or queen lives and works: *We received an invitation to the king's court.* ◄——— **Example sentence**

Definitions

court 2 *v* **1** to try to make someone one like you: *The senator will court voters before the election.* **2** to do something that makes a problem likely to happen: *Martin is courting disaster if he goes to the movies instead of studying for his exam.* **3** to try to win the romantic love of someone: *Andrew courted Susan with flowers and candy.*

——— **Example Sentence**

Dictionary pages also have other helpful information.

Guide words are at the top of dictionary pages. They tell you the first or the last entry on the page. Guide words can help you find words in a dictionary.

Words can be divided into **syllables,** or parts.

A stress mark (') shows which syllable in a word to **stress**—to pronounce stronger and louder.

Many dictionaries include **illustrations** to help explain the meanings of some words.

An **idiom** is two or more words that have a special meaning when used together. Dictionaries explain what each idiom means. Note that each idiom including the word *hang* has a different meaning.

handle² *verb* (**handling, handled**)
1 to hold or touch something: *Handle the package with care.*
2 to control or deal with someone or something: *I can't handle the children by myself.*

han•dle•bars /ˈhændl,barz/ *plural noun*
the parts of a bicycle that you hold when you ride it

hand•some /ˈhænsəm/ *adjective*
attractive, usually used about a man compare ▶▶BEAUTIFUL

hand•writ•ing /ˈhænd,raɪṭɪŋ/ *noun* [U]
the way someone writes with his or her hand: *He has very neat handwriting.*

hand•y /ˈhændi/ *adjective* (**handier, handiest**)
1 useful: *A second car comes in handy sometimes.*
2 near: *Keep the medicine handy in case we need it.*

*He **hung** the clothes out to dry.*

hang /hæŋ/ *verb*
1 (*past* **hung** /hʌŋ/) to fasten something at the top so that the bottom part is free to move: *I hung up my coat in the closet.*
2 (*past* **hanged**) to kill someone by holding him or her above the ground with a rope around his or her neck
3 **hang around** to stay in one place and do nothing, or to wait around for someone: *He was hanging around outside my house.*
4 **hang on** to hold something tightly: *Hang on to your hat, it's very windy.*
5 **hang out** to stay in one place and not do very much: *We usually hang out at Jill's house after school.*
6 **hang up** to finish speaking to someone on the telephone by putting the telephone down

hang•er /ˈhæŋɚ/ *noun*
a curved piece of wire or wood that you hang clothes on

MAPS

Maps help us learn more about our world. They show the location of places such as countries, states, and cities. Some maps show where mountains, rivers, and lakes are located.

Maps usually have helpful features. For example, a **compass rose** shows which way is north. A **scale** shows how miles or kilometers are represented on the map.

▲ Routes of the Underground Railroad

Street maps help give directions within a city or town. They tell how to go from one place to another. Look at the map of New Orleans. Can you find the Public Library? What streets is it near?

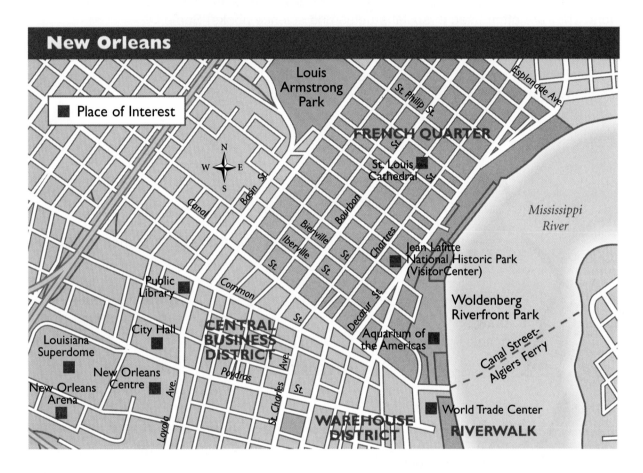

New Orleans

Place of Interest

Louis Armstrong Park

Esplanade Ave.

St. Philip St.

FRENCH QUARTER

St. Louis Cathedral

Mississippi River

N
W E
S

Basin St.

Canal St.

Bienville St.

Iberville St.

Bourbon St.

Chartres

Jean Lafitte National Historic Park (Visitor Center)

Woldenberg Riverfront Park

Public Library

Common St.

CENTRAL BUSINESS DISTRICT

Decatur St.

Aquarium of the Americas

Canal Street-Algiers Ferry

City Hall

Louisiana Superdome

New Orleans Centre

Poydras St.

St. Charles Ave.

St. Charles St.

World Trade Center

New Orleans Arena

Loyola Ave.

WAREHOUSE DISTRICT

RIVERWALK

DIAGRAMS

Diagrams are drawings or plans used to explain things or show how things work. They are often used in social studies and science books. Some diagrams show pictures of how objects look on the outside or on the inside. Others show the different steps in a process.

This diagram shows the steps of the Scientific Method. It helps you understand the order and importance of each step.

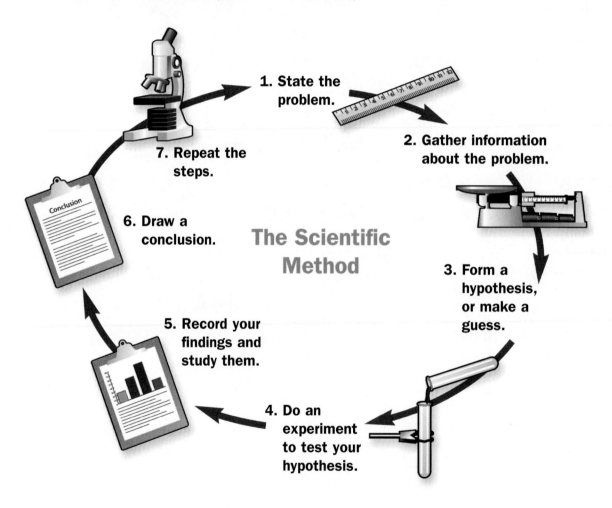

The Scientific Method

1. State the problem.

2. Gather information about the problem.

3. Form a hypothesis, or make a guess.

4. Do an experiment to test your hypothesis.

5. Record your findings and study them.

6. Draw a conclusion.

7. Repeat the steps.

CROSS-SECTION DIAGRAMS

A **cross-section diagram** shows what something looks like on the inside. This diagram shows the stored food and the plant embryo inside a kernel of corn.

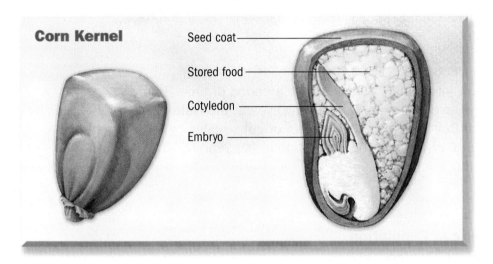

Corn Kernel

Seed coat
Stored food
Cotyledon
Embryo

FLOWCHARTS

A **flowchart** is a diagram that uses shapes and arrows to show a step-by-step process. The flowchart below shows the steps involved in making spaghetti. Each arrow points to the next step.

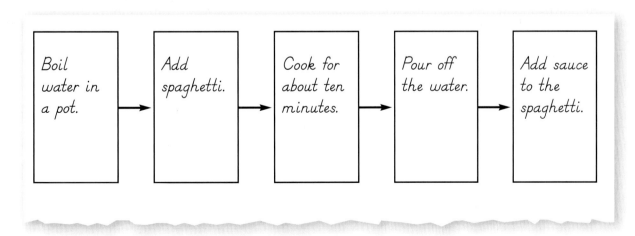

Boil water in a pot. → Add spaghetti. → Cook for about ten minutes. → Pour off the water. → Add sauce to the spaghetti.

GRAPHS

Graphs organize and explain information. They show how two or more kinds of information are related, or how they are alike. Graphs are often used in math, science, and social studies books. Three common kinds of graphs are **line graphs, bar graphs,** and **circle graphs.**

LINE GRAPHS

A **line graph** shows how information changes over a period of time. This line graph explains how, over a period of about 100 years, the Native American population of Central Mexico decreased, or got smaller, by more than 20 million people. Can you find the population in the year 1540? In 1580?

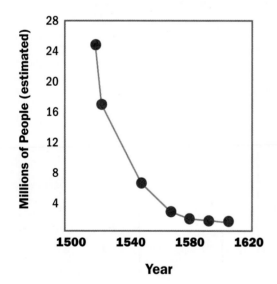

Native American Population of Central Mexico

BAR GRAPHS

We use **bar graphs** to compare information. For example, this bar graph compares the populations of the thirteen United States in 1790. It shows that, in 1790, Virginia had over ten times as many people as Delaware.

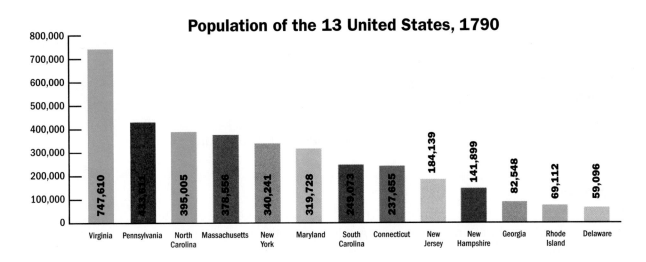

Population of the 13 United States, 1790

CIRCLE GRAPHS

A **circle graph** is sometimes called a pie chart because it looks like a pie cut into slices, or pieces. Circle graphs are used to show how different parts of a whole thing compare to each other. In a circle graph, all the "slices" add up to 100 percent. This circle graph shows that only 29 percent of the earth's surface is land. It also shows that the continent of Asia takes up 30 percent of the earth's land.

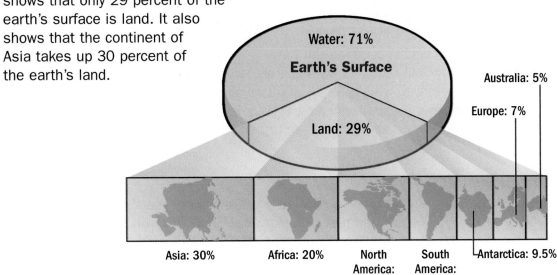

Writing Process Handbook

Writing allows you to express what you think and to share information. The **Writing Process** is a series of steps that can help you write clearly and effectively.

STEP 1: PREWRITE

Writers have to begin somewhere. **Prewriting** is a good way to start. In this step, you collect topic ideas, choose a topic, plan your writing, and gather information.

LIST TOPIC IDEAS
You need ideas before you can begin writing. One way to get ideas is to **brainstorm**. Brainstorming means writing a list of all the topic ideas you can think of.

CHOOSE A TOPIC
Look at your list of topic ideas. Choose the one that is most interesting. This is your **topic,** the subject you will write about.

PLAN YOUR WRITING
Plan your writing by following these steps:
- First, decide on the type of writing that works best with your topic. For example, you may want to write a description, a story, or a personal narrative. The type of writing is called the **form** of writing.
- Then, think about who will read your writing. This is the **audience.** It will help you decide whether to write formally or informally.
- Finally, decide what your reason for writing is. This is your **purpose.** Is your purpose to inform your audience? To entertain them? To tell them your opinion?

GATHER INFORMATION
The way you gather information depends on what you are writing. For example, for a report, you need to do research. For a movie review, you might list what you liked and didn't like about the movie. For a description, you might write your ideas in a chart.

270

Here is a chart a student named Rebecca made for her description of her cat. She listed her ideas in the Supporting Details boxes.

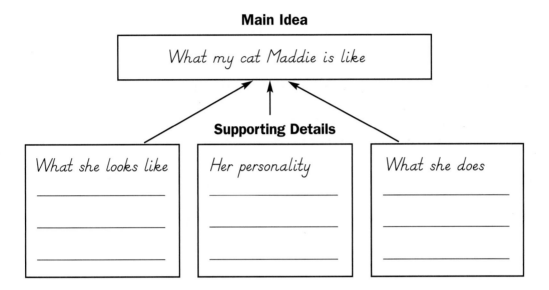

Main Idea

What my cat Maddie is like

Supporting Details

| What she looks like | Her personality | What she does |

STEP 2: DRAFT

In this step, you start writing. Don't worry too much about spelling and punctuation. Your first draft doesn't have to be perfect. Just put your ideas into sentences.

Here is the first paragraph that Rebecca wrote for her first draft.

> Maddie is a pretty cat. Her body is mostly white. There are brown spots on her face and tail. She has big blue eyes and long white whiskers. Maddie has a black spot under her nose. It looks like half a mustache.

STEP 3: EDIT

Now it's time to edit, or make changes. To edit your writing, follow these steps: review, consult, and mark corrections.

REVIEW YOUR DRAFT
Read over your first draft. As you read, ask yourself these questions:
- Are my ideas presented in the best order?
- Is there a beginning, a middle, and an end?
- Does each paragraph have a main idea and supporting details?

CONSULT OTHERS
When you edit, it helps to get someone's opinion. You can have a **peer review.** In a peer review, you ask a classmate to read your writing and to write questions or comments about it. Your classmate's comments can help you decide what you need to change.

MARK CORRECTIONS
Once you know what you want to change, you can mark the corrections on your first draft. Use the **editing marks** in the chart.

Editing Marks		
To:	**Use This Mark:**	**Example:**
add something	$\wedge$	We ate rice, bean$_\wedge^s$ and corn.
delete something	ℛ	We ate rice, beans, and corns.
start a new paragraph	¶	¶ We ate rice, beans, and corn.
add a comma	$_\wedge^,$	We ate rice, beans and corn.
add a period	⊙	We ate rice, beans, and corn⊙
switch letters or words	∽	We ate rice, baens, and corn.
change to a capital letter	$\underset{\equiv}{a}$	we ate rice, beans, and corn.
change to a lowercase letter	Ⱥ	WE ate rice, beans, and corn.

272

Here's how Rebecca marked up her first paragraph.

> really beautiful
> Maddie is a ~~pretty~~ cat. Her body is mostly white, but There are
>   ,
> brown spots on her face and tail. She has big blue eyes and long
>   so
> white whiskers. Maddie has a black spot under her nose, It looks
>   ,
>   she has
> like half a mustache.

STEP 4: REVISE

In this step, you write a new draft that includes the changes you marked on your first draft. Then check your work and make final corrections.

WRITE YOUR SECOND DRAFT

Make all of the corrections you marked on your first draft. You can also add details you may have thought of since writing your first draft.

Here's Rebecca's first paragraph after she finished revising it.

> My favorite pet is my cat Maddie. Maddie is a really beautiful cat. Her body is mostly white, but there are brown spots on her face and tail. She has big blue eyes and long white whiskers. Maddie has a black spot under her nose, so it looks like she has half a mustache.

CHECK YOUR WORK AND MAKE FINAL CORRECTIONS

Reread your paper. Check for mistakes in spelling and punctuation. Correct any mistakes you find. Your writing is now ready for others to read.

Here is Rebecca's finished paper.

My Cat Maddie

My favorite pet is my cat Maddie. Maddie is a really beautiful cat. Her body is mostly white, but there are brown spots on her face and tail. She has big blue eyes and long white whiskers. Maddie has a black spot under her nose, so it looks like she has half a mustache.

Maddie has a great personality. She is very friendly. She likes to purr a lot, especially when I scratch behind her ears. She often sits on my lap when I'm watching TV or reading a book. Maddie is also very playful. Her favorite toy is a mouse. When I give her the mouse, she hits it and runs around the house. That always makes me laugh.

Sometimes Maddie is too playful. For example, she jumps on the table when my family is eating. Then my Dad yells, "Maddie! Go down!" Then she jumps off the table and runs away. She also likes to jump on the bed and play with my toes when I am sleeping. Then I take her out of the bedroom.

I am always happy to see Maddie when I get home from school. To me, she is the greatest cat in the world.

STEP 5: PUBLISH

Once your paper is revised and proofread, share it with others. Look at these publishing tips.

PUBLISHING TIPS

- Photocopy and hand out your work to your classmates.
- Attach it to an e-mail and send it to friends.
- Send it to a school newspaper or magazine for possible publication.

Once you've shared your work with others, you may want to keep it in a **portfolio,** a folder or envelope with your other writing. It's a good idea to organize the work in your portfolio by date.

Each time you write something, add it to your portfolio. Compare recent work with earlier work. See if your writing is improving. See if you have difficulty with some things. If so, focus on these things next time you are writing. That's how writers improve.

Glossary

ADJECTIVE /aj′ik tiv/
An adjective describes a noun—a person, place, or thing: *I have a blue car.* An adjective can also describe a pronoun: *She is tall.*

ADVERB /ad′vėrb/
An adverb usually describes the action of a verb. It tells how an action happens: *The boy runs quickly.*

ARTICLE /är′ti kəl/
An article is a word that identifies a noun. Use *a* or *an* to talk about one general person, place, or thing: *I eat a peach or an apple every day.* Use *the* to talk about one or more specific persons, places, or things: *The dog is brown.*

AUTOBIOGRAPHY /ȯ′tə bī og′rə fē/
An autobiography is the story of the writer's own life, told by the writer. It may tell about the person's whole life or only a part of it. Autobiographies are nonfiction.

BASE FORM /bās fôrm/
The base form of a verb has no added ending (-*s*, -*ing*, -*ed*). *Talk* is the base form of the verb *talk*. (Other forms of *talk* are *talks*, *talking*, and *talked*.)

BIOGRAPHICAL NARRATIVE
/bī′ə graf′i kəl nar′ə tiv/
A biographical narrative is the true story of a real person's life. Writers often tell the events of a biographical narrative in chronological order, or the order in which they happened.

BRAINSTORMING /brān′stôr′ming/
Brainstorming is writing down all the ideas you can think of about a subject or topic as quickly as possible. You can brainstorm alone or with other people.

CAPTION /kap′shən/
A caption is the text written under or next to a photograph, picture, or diagram. A caption explains what the photograph, picture, or diagram shows.

CAUSE AND EFFECT /kȯz and ə fekt′/
Why something happens is a cause. What happens is an effect. When you read a text, look for causes and effects. Finding causes and effects as you read can help you better understand a text.

CHARACTER /kar′ik tər/
A character is a person or an animal in a story.

CHRONOLOGICAL ORDER (TIME ORDER)
/kron′ə loj′i kəl ôrd′ər/
Chronological order, or time order, is the order in which events happen in a story. To tell story events in chronological order, writers use time phrases such as *in 1976, on May 1,* and *the next year.*

COMPARATIVE FORM OF ADJECTIVES
/kəm par′ə tiv fôrm ov aj′ik tivz/
Use the comparative form of an adjective to compare two people, places, or things. For most one-syllable adjectives, add -*er* + *than*: *Bigger than* is the comparative form of *big*. For two-syllable adjectives that end in -*y*, change the *y* to *i* and add -*er* + *than*: *Prettier than* is the comparative form of *pretty*. For most two-syllable adjectives, use *more* + adjective + *than*: *More famous than* is the comparative form of *famous*.

COMPARISON /kəm par′ə sən/
A comparison tells how two or more people, places, or things are alike and different.

COMPOUND SENTENCE
/kom′pound sen′təns/
A compound sentence is made up of two or more simple sentences, or independent clauses: *I went to the store, and Joe went to the gym.*

CONJUNCTION /kən jungk′shən/
A conjunction joins words, groups of words, and whole sentences. The words *and*, *but*, *so*, *or*, *nor*, *for*, and *yet* are conjunctions.

CONTRACTION /kən trak′shən/
A contraction is a word made from two words that have been joined together. An apostrophe shows where a letter or letters have been taken away. For example, the contraction of *I am* is *I'm*. Contractions are common in speaking and informal writing.

DESCRIPTION /di skrip′shən/
A description is a form of writing. Writers use adjectives and sensory images to help their readers see, hear, taste, feel, or smell whatever they are describing.

DIAGRAM /dī′ə gram/
A diagram is a picture or a plan that gives information in a visual way. Diagrams can help readers understand a text. Science and social studies books often have diagrams. Examples of diagrams include a labeled drawing of parts of a flower and a floor plan of a house.

DRAW CONCLUSIONS
/drȯ kən klü′zhənz/
To draw a conclusion means to decide something is true based on information. For example, you see a young person carrying a book bag. You may draw the conclusion that the person is a student.

FABLE /fā′bəl/
A fable is a brief story, usually with animal characters that speak and act like humans. A fable often teaches a moral, or lesson.

FICTION /fik′shən/
Fiction is writing that tells about imaginary characters and events. Short stories and novels are works of fiction.

FOLKTALE /fōk′tāl/
A folktale is a story that people, or folk, told one another by word of mouth over many generations. In time, people wrote down the stories so that they would not be forgotten.

FREEWRITING /frē′rī ting/
Freewriting is writing down your ideas, thoughts, and feelings as quickly as you can. Freewriting can sometimes help you get ideas for other forms of writing.

IMPERATIVE /im per′ət iv/
We use the imperative to give directions or orders. The subject of an imperative sentence is usually *you*. The subject is usually not stated: *(You) Open your books to page 5.*

INFORMATIONAL TEXT
/in′fər mā′shən əl tekst/
Informational text is nonfiction text. It presents facts and other information about real people, events, places, and situations.

IRONY /ī′rə nē/

When the reader knows something about a situation in a story that a character in the story does not know, the writer has used irony. Writers use irony to make a story humorous and to teach us about life.

JOURNAL /jėr′nəl/

A journal is a book that a person writes in. People write in journals to record their thoughts and feelings about things that happen in their lives. Each separate writing in a journal is called an entry. A journal entry is personal and informal.

LEGEND /lĕj′ənd/

A legend is a story that people tell and retell over many, many years. Legends often change over time.

LETTER /lĕt′ər/

A letter is a written communication from one person to another. In a personal letter, the writer shares information and ideas with a family member or close friend.

MAIN IDEAS AND DETAILS

/mān ī dē′ əz ənd dē′tālz/

The main ideas are the biggest or most important ideas in a text. Details are facts or examples that support the main ideas.

MAKE INFERENCES /māk in′fər əns əs/

Sometimes writers do not tell you what a story means. Instead, they give you clues. The clues can be things that the characters do and say. You use the clues to make inferences, or guesses, about the story's meaning.

MYTH /mith/

A myth is a fictional story. Long ago, groups of people created myths to explain natural events. Parents told the myths to their children, and the myths passed from generation to generation. Myths are part of a group's spoken tradition.

NARRATIVE /nar′ə tiv/

A narrative is a story. It can be either fiction or nonfiction. Novels and short stories are fictional narratives. Biographies and autobiographies are nonfictional narratives, or true stories. A personal narrative tells about an experience in the writer's life. A biographical narrative tells the true story of a real person's life.

NARRATOR /nar′ā tər/

A narrator is a speaker or character who tells a story. The narrator sometimes takes part in the action. Other times the narrator just speaks about the action.

NONFICTION /non fik′shən/

Nonfiction is true information. It tells about real people, places, objects, or events. Biographies, reports, and newspaper articles are examples of nonfiction.

NOUN /noun/

A noun is the name of a person, place, or thing. Examples of common nouns are *plane*, *building*, and *child*. Examples of proper nouns are *Robert*, *Chicago*, and *Puerto Rico*.

OBJECT PRONOUN /ob′jikt prō′noun/

An object pronoun (*me, you, him, her, it, us, you, them*) replaces a noun that is the object of a sentence: *Bob knows me.*

PARAGRAPH /par′ə graf/

A paragraph is a group of sentences about one idea in a piece of writing.

PERSONAL NARRATIVE
/pər′sən əl nar′ə tiv/

A personal narrative is a story about an experience in the writer's life. A writer usually tells a personal narrative in chronological order.

PLAY /plā/

A play is a story that actors usually perform on a stage in a theater. Although plays are meant to be performed, actors can also read aloud the written version, called a script.

PLOT /plot/

A plot is what happens in a story. In most stories, the plot has characters and a main problem or conflict. The plot usually begins with information to help the reader understand the story. Then an event introduces the main problem. The problem grows until there is a turning point, or climax, when a character tries to solve the problem. The events after the climax lead to the end of the story.

POEM /pō′əm/

A poem is a piece of writing. Poems use patterns of words and sounds to express ideas, experiences, and emotions. Poems are written in lines.

PREDICT /pri dikt′/

To predict means to guess what will happen. When you read, try to look for clues in the story and in the pictures. Think about what will happen next. When you are finished reading, see if your predictions were correct.

PREPOSITION /prep′ə zish′ən/

A preposition is a connecting word that shows time, place, or direction. *After*, *above*, *across*, *to*, and *at* are prepositions: *We went to the store.*

PREPOSITIONAL PHRASE
/prep′ə zish′ə nəl frāz/

A prepositional phrase starts with a preposition and ends with a noun or pronoun: *My family lives in the city*.

PREVIEWING /prē′vyüing/

Previewing a text means looking at the pages before you start to read. Previewing includes looking at the headings in dark type as well as the pictures and maps.

PRONOUN /prō′noun/

A pronoun is a word that takes the place of a noun: *Nadia goes to school. She likes it. She* replaces the proper noun *Nadia*; *it* replaces the noun *school*.

PROSE /prōz/

Prose is the ordinary language people use in speaking and writing. Most writing that is not poetry, drama, or song is considered prose. Prose occurs in two forms: fiction and nonfiction.

PUNCTUATION /pungk′chü ā′shən/

Punctuation is the system of using certain signs or marks, such as periods (.) and commas(,), to divide writing into phrases and sentences so that the meaning is clear. Besides periods and commas, common punctuation marks include exclamation points (!), question marks (?), hyphens (-), semicolons (;), and colons (:).

REPORT /ri pôrt´/
A report is a piece of writing about a topic. You can organize information for a report by writing notes.

SENSORY IMAGES /sĕn´ sə rē im´ij iz/
Sensory images are words that appeal to one or more of the five senses. Sensory images are like word pictures. They help readers to see, hear, taste, touch, or smell things in a poem or other literary text.

SENTENCE /sen´təns/
A sentence is a group of words with a subject and a verb. A sentence expresses a complete thought.

SEQUENCE OF EVENTS
/sē´kwəns ov i vents´/
A sequence, or order, of events is a series of related actions that has a particular result. In both fiction and nonfiction writing, the sequence of events is often in chronological order.

SEQUENCE WORDS /sē´kwəns wėrdz´/
Sequence words help make the order of steps or events clear. Some common sequence words are *first, second, next, then, after that,* and *finally*: *First, you should finish your homework. After that, you may go outside.*

SETTING /set´ing/
The setting of a literary text is the time and place of the action. In most stories, the setting is where the characters interact. Setting can also help create a feeling, or atmosphere.

SHORT STORY /shôrt stôr´ē/
A short story is a short work of fiction. A short story usually presents a sequence of events, or a plot, and has a clear beginning, middle, and end. One or more characters usually has a problem or conflict. A short story usually presents a message about life.

SIMILE /sim´ə lē/
A simile is a figure of speech that uses the word *like* to compare two different things in an unusual way: *Her hair was like spun gold.*

SIMPLE PAST TENSE /sim´pəl past tens/
Use the simple past tense to talk about completed actions in the past. For regular verbs, add -*ed* to the base form: *The girl walked up the hill.* Other verbs have irregular past-tense forms: *The boy ate the apple.*

SONG /song/
A song is a piece of music with words.

STRATEGY /strat´ə jē/
A tool or a plan you can use to achieve a goal or learn to do something better.

SUBJECT PRONOUN /sub´jikt prō´noun/
A subject pronoun (*I, you, he, she, it, we, you, they*) replaces a noun that is the subject of a sentence: *Roberto goes to school. He takes the bus.*

SUBJECT-VERB AGREEMENT
/sub´jikt vėrb ə grē´mənt/
In the simple present, the subject and verb of a sentence must agree. When the subject is a singular noun or *he, she,* or *it*, add -*s* or -*es* to the noun: *A man runs.* When a verb ends in -*y*, change the *y* to *i* and add -*es*: *The dog carries his bone.* When the subject is a plural noun or *I, you, we,* or *they*, use the base form of the verb: *The men run.* Do not add -*s* or -*es*.

SUMMARIZE /sum′ə rīz/
To summarize means to write the main ideas of a text in your own words. As you read a text, summarize each section. Be sure to keep your summaries simple. When you are finished reading, reread your summaries. This will help you understand and remember main ideas.

TIME PHRASE /tīm frāz/
Time phrases tell the reader when an event happened: *Yesterday, we went to see a movie. Next week, we will go to see my grandmother.*

TIMELINE /tīm′ līn/
A timeline is a diagram that shows important dates and the order of events in history.

VERB /vėrb/
A verb expresses action (*swims, drives*) or being (for example, *is*): *Tom swims fast* (action). *Sally is very sick* (being).

VISUALIZING /vizh′ü ə līz′ing/
Visualizing is picturing something in your mind.

WRITING PROCESS /rī′ting pro′ses/
The writing process is a series of steps to help you write. Many writers use the writing process to think of ideas and then to organize, write, and revise their ideas. The steps are: Prewrite, Draft, Edit, Revise, and Publish.

Index

Acknowledgments

Cherry Lane Music Publishing Company, Inc. (ASCAP) and DreamWorks Songs (ASCAP). "Garden Song," words and music by Dave Mallett. Copyright © 1975 Cherry Lane Music Publishing Company, Inc. (ASCAP) and DreamWorks Songs (ASCAP). Worldwide rights for DreamWorks Songs administered by Cherry Lane Music Publishing Company, Inc. International copyright secured. All rights reserved.

HarperCollins Publishers, Inc. "Aaron's Gift," adapted from "Aaron's Gift" from *The Witch of Fourth Street and Other Stories*, text copyright © 1972 by Myron Levoy. Published by Harper & Row, New York.

Pie Corbett. "Wings" by Pie Corbett. Reprinted by permission of the author.

Paterson Marsh Ltd. "Rain Poem" by Elizabeth Coatsworth. Reprinted by permission of Paterson Marsh Ltd. on behalf of The Estate of Elizabeth Coatsworth.

Dan Scanlan. "Giant Silent Redwood" by Dan Scanlan. Copyright © 1996.

Scholastic Press. "This Big Sky" by Pat Mora, from *This Big Sky* by Pat Mora. Reprinted by permission of Scholastic Press, an imprint of Scholastic Inc.

Credits

Illustrators: **Esther Baran** 133–136, 138; **Liz Callen** 146–150, 175, 263; **Oki Han** 44–48, 50; **John Hovell** 7, 9, 10, 265, 266, 269; **Inklink Firenze** 12, 23, 25, 100, 102–106, 108, 267; **Tom Leonard** 113, 115, 169, 171, 172, 173, 201; **Mapping Specialists** 70, 264; **Gail Piazza** xiii, 205–211, 216; **Roger Roth** 73; **Tony Smith** 59–62, 64–65; **Arvis Stewart** 21, 39, 40, 58, 80, 83, 88, 102, 124, 132, 146, 176–180, 182, 190, 204.

Photography:

COVER: Panel top, Dorling Kindersley; middle, CORBIS/Bettmann; bottom, Omni Photo Communications; bottom, Museum of Flight/CORBIS; background, David Muench/CORBIS; inset left, Gianni Dagli Orti/CORBIS; inset right, Liu Liqun/CORBIS.

INTRO UNIT: 2 panel top left, Dorling Kindersley; 2 panel middle left, Getty Images; 2 panel middle left, CORBIS; 2 panel bottom left, Getty Images; 2 bottom left, Getty Images; 2-3 Tom Stewart/CORBIS; 3 inset, Dorling Kindersley; 3 bottom, Ariel Skelley/CORBIS; 4 left, Dorling Kindersley; 4 right, Paul Conklin/Photo Edit; 5 Michael Heron/CORBIS; 6 left, CORBIS; 6 right, Dennis MacDonald/Photo Edit; 8 left, CORBIS; 8 right, Jonathan Nourok/Photo Edit; 9 bottom, Bill Bachmann/The Image Works; 10 top, David Young-Wolff/Photo Edit; 11 Michael Newman/Photo Edit; 12 left, Reed Kaestner/CORBIS; 12 right, Getty Images; 13 Cleve Bryant/Photo Edit; 14 Kooyman/Animals Animals; 15 Getty Images; 16 top, David Young-Wolff/Photo Edit; 16 middle, Getty Images; 16 bottom, Dorling Kindersley; 17 Lou Wall/CORBIS; 18 US Geological Survey; 19 all, Getty Images; 20 Getty Images; 22 all, Getty Images; 24 left, Dorling Kindersley; 24 middle, CORBIS; 24 right, Dorling Kindersley; 25 all, Dorling Kindersley; 27 Dorling Kindersley; 29 top, Paul Katz/Index Stock Imagery; 29 bottom left & right, Pearson Learning; 30 Prentice Hall School Division; 31 Prentice Hall School Division; 32 Getty Images; 33 top, Spencer Grant/Photo Edit; 33 bottom, Tony Freeman/Photo Edit.

UNIT 1: 34 panel top left, Dorling Kindersley; 34 panel middle left, Dorling Kindersley; 34 bottom left, Kevin Flemming/CORBIS; 34-35, Firefly Productions/CORBIS; 35 inset, Dorling Kindersley; 35 bottom, Dorling Kindersley; 36 left, John Van Hasselt/CORBIS Sygma; 36 right, Getty Images; 37 top left, Dorling Kindersley; 37 right, Dorling Kindersley; 37 bottom left, Robert Holmes/CORBIS; 38 left, Keren Su/Getty Images; 38 right, Archivo Iconographico, S.A./CORBIS; 39 bottom, Dorling Kindersley; 40 top, Superstock; 40 bottom, Jeannine Davis-Kimball; 41 top left, Robert Holmes/CORBIS; 41 top right, Dorling Kindersley; 41 middle, Dorling Kindersley; 41 bottom left, Wolfgang Kaehler/CORBIS; 41 bottom right, Dorling Kindersley; 42, Peter Harholdt/CORBIS; 43 all, Dorling Kindersley; 51 top, Dorling Kindersley; 51 bottom, EMG Education Management Group; 52, Dorling Kindersley.

Researchers; 159 top, Gallo Images/CORBIS; 159 bottom, B. Borrell Casals; Frank Lane Picture Agency/CORBIS; 160 Dorling Kindersley; 188, Arthur Morris/CORBIS; 162 Dorling Kindersley; 163 Ralph A. Reinhold/Animals, Animals; 164 Dorling Kindersley.

UNIT 7: 166 panel top left, Omni Photo Communications; 166 panel middle left, Getty Images; 166 panel bottom left, Holt Studios Ltd.; 166 bottom, William Dow/CORBIS; 166-167 Jim Zuckerman/CORBIS; 167 inset, Robert A. Tyrell Photography; 167 bottom, Bettmann/CORBIS; 168 top, Michael Fogden/DRK Photo; 168 bottom, Getty Images; 169 Joel Greenstein/Omni Photo Communications; 170 top, Dorling Kindersley; 170-171 Getty Images; 170 bottom, Robert Frerck/Getty Images; 171 Phil Schermeister/CORBIS; 172 Oxford Scientific Films/Animals, Animals; 173 top, Dorling Kindersley; 173 bottom, Stephen Oliver/Dorling Kindersley; 174 Dorling Kindersley; 177 Benvie/Animals Animals; 183 Sally A. Morgan/Ecoscene /CORBIS; 185 top, David Nunuk/Science Photo Library/Photo Researchers; 185 bottom, Getty Images.

UNIT 8: 188 panel top left, Museum of Flight/CORBIS; 188 panel top middle, Arthur Morris/CORBIS; 188 panel top bottom, Swim Ink/CORBIS; 188 bottom, Bettmann/ CORBIS; 188 inset, Dorling Kindersley; 188-189 Bruce Burkhardt/CORBIS; 189 inset, Imperial War Museum; 189 bottom, Getty Images; 191 left, Underwood & Underwood/CORBIS; 191 top right, Schomburg Center for Research in Black Culture/The New York Public Library; 191 bottom right, United States Postal Service; 192 top, Smithsonian Institution; 192 bottom, Bettmann/CORBIS; 193 top, CORBIS; 193 bottom, Hulton-Deutsch Collection/CORBIS; 194 top, Smithsonian Institution; 194 middle, Smithsonian Institution; 194 bottom, Dorling Kindersley; 195 top, Library of Congress; 195 bottom left, United States Postal Service; 195 bottom right, Bettmann/CORBIS; 197 Index Stock Imagery; 198 Kennan Ward/CORBIS; 199 Dorling Kindersley; 203 Dorling Kindersley; 212 Lawrence Migdale; 213 Getty Images; 214 top, Smithsonian Institution; 214 bottom, Bettmann/CORBIS; 215 Swim Ink/CORBIS; 219 Getty Images; 223 Getty Images; 224 top, Getty Images; 224 bottom, The Gorilla Foundation/Ron Cohn.

HANDBOOK: 274 Rebecca Ortman; 274 Will Hart.